Beginner's
Fabric Dyeing and Printing

Beginner's Guides are available on the following subjects

Audio
Building Construction
Cameras
Central Heating
Colour Television
Computers
Digital Electronics
Domestic Plumbing
Electric Wiring
Electronics
Gemmology
Home Energy Saving
Integrated Circuits
Microprocessors
Photography
Processing and Printing
Radio
Spinning
Super-8 Film Making
Tape Recording
Technical Illustration
Television
Transistors
Video
Weaving
Woodturning
Woodworking

Beginner's Guide to
Fabric Dyeing and Printing

Stuart and Patricia Robinson

Newnes Technical Books

Newnes Technical Books

is an imprint of the Butterworth Group
which has principal offices in
London, Boston, Durban, Singapore, Sydney, Toronto, Wellington

First published 1982

British Library Cataloguing in Publication Data
Robinson, Stuart
    Beginner's guide to fabric dying and printing.
    1. Dyes and dyeing, Domestic
    2. Textile printing
    I. Title   II. Robinson, Patricia
    746.6   TT853

    ISBN 0-408-00575-0

Photoset by Butterworths Litho Preparation Department
Printed in England by Whitstable Litho Ltd, Whitstable, Kent

Preface

The decoration of textiles by dyeing or printing is basically a simple matter. It can be made more complicated, but elaborate techniques are not necessary to the production of useful and decorative fabrics of a very high standard of craftsmanship and design.

This book aims to present in simple language the basic techniques and materials available to the amateur working at home, or in school or college, with the minimum of space, materials, and equipment.

In the past, techniques were often complex, requiring much skill and dyes that were often difficult to obtain, but the present-day dyes available to beginners are in good supply, relatively simple to use, and, in the main, fast to light and washing. Techniques, too, are less complicated, needing simpler apparatus and methods.

This simplification, which has occurred in the past decade, also permits a much more experimental approach to design. Ideas and patterns can be developed on the fabric rather than by attempting to make the pattern on the textile conform exactly to a design upon paper. Too often such an approach results in a pattern which does not appear as an integral part of the fabric but rather as a superimposed decoration, worked out in one medium and merely transferred, with little adjustment, to another.

Fabric, design, textures, and dyestuffs must be used with an open, enquiring mind. Although textiles can be used flat or folded, worn, hung, or draped, it is most important that the pattern, if it is true to the nature of the fabric, appears to be an integral part of the cloth.

The hand craftsman cannot hope to achieve the perfectly matched repeats possible with machines. This, however, is the craftsman's great asset, as it enables him to achieve lively, individual artefacts bearing a personal stamp impossible in mass-produced work. Each technique shown in this book has its own 'mystery', and the wise craftsman will not try to imitate one – say batik – with another, such as screen printing. Each technique develops its own way of working and, within its limits, each can be most satisfying and rewarding. It is intended that the ideas presented will serve as sources of inspiration and not merely as blueprints to be imitated.

We wish to thank the following for their co-operation and practical help in the preparation of samples. E. J. Arnold & Son Ltd., Leeds; Dylon International Ltd., London; George Rowney & Co. Ltd., Bracknell; Sericol Group Ltd., London; Whaleys (Bradford) Ltd.; Siphon Art, Ignacio, California.

The cover photograph shows a mercerised cotton length patterned with a tjanting and dyed in mixed Dylon Cold Water Dyes. Silk cushion cover tied and dyed in acid dyes. Dyeing by Patricia Robinson.

S. & P. R.

Contents

1

Introduction

The exact origins of textile dyeing and dye-patterning lie in antiquity, when contemporary written records did not exist, and the fabrics have long perished. It is not until the ancient Babylonians and Assyrians that we find sculptured representations of patterned garments in wall sculptures. Clay tablets from Ur around 2200 B.C. record the presence of weavers and dyers. It is surmised that the early development of dyes among primitive peoples consisted of trial and error, successful recipes being handed down by word of mouth. Progress must have been very slow, with many mistakes and missed opportunities. It is known that in remote times China, India, and Persia had achieved flourishing textile industries for their own use and export.

By late mediaeval times, the trades of weaver and dyer in Europe had formed their own guilds, which controlled methods and materials with the utmost severity. High standards of dyeing were maintained, using local dyestuffs, to which were gradually added imported dyes, mordants, and chemicals from the Far East and the New World as explorers and merchants sought out new markets.

In the middle of the 19th century, mauveine was the first of a long series of dyes manufactured from coal tar which heralded other classes of dyestuffs and dyeing processes. These have largely superseded natural dyes, just as manmade fibres have in the main replaced many natural fibres.

Block printing, it has been suggested, was known in India in 3000 B.C., although no blocks or textiles have survived.

Direct evidence does not appear until the 4th century B.C. Printed textiles and blocks from graves at Achmin, the ancient city of Panopolis, in Upper Egypt are some of the earliest still in existence.

Block printing continued until the invention of flat copper plates in the late 18th century, followed by rotary or roller printing, which remained in use until well into the 20th century. In the late 19th century, screen printing was developed and is now the technique most widely used in the production of fabrics. At first, flat screens were used, but since 1945 rotary screens have been developed with larger outputs and more mechanised control.

Other developments have included transfer printing and polychromatic dyeing.

2

Equipment

Although a great deal of experimental and small work can be carried out without elaborate or expensive equipment, serious, large-scale work on repeat-pattern lengths or hangings will require the careful planning of the working area to permit the progression of differing techniques. It is particularly important to separate clean and dirty areas so as to provide somewhere well away from the dyeing, printing, or waxing work spaces where fabrics can hang while drying, fixing, etc.

The techniques described in this book require a sink and a supply of cold water, and a source of heat, such as a gas or electric ring, preferably near the sink.

The printing table

The minimum working surface is a sturdy, flat-topped table. This could be a simple kitchen table or one specially made. The essentials are that it has a flat surface and is well constructed. A free-standing table that enables one to work from all sides is preferable.

Where the table is required for other household use, a loose working cover can be made from a piece of 12 mm (½ in) or thicker chipboard, blockboard, or plywood with a frame around the underneath edge. The frame will steady the cover and hold it on the tabletop during printing. At other times, it can be stored elsewhere (*Figure 2.1*).

For tie-and-dye and batik work, the tabletop should be covered with a piece of plastic sheeting or an opened-out

3

large plastic bag. For pad, block, and screen printing, the tabletop will require some padding, such as a blanket or piece of carpet underfelt, that is even, flat, and has no joins, holes, or bumps in it, similarly covered with a piece of plastic (*Figure 2.2*).

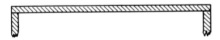

Figure 2.1. A loose working top (section)

For serious work in block and screen printing, a special table, designed to give the maximum quality of print and to be easy to maintain, is essential. It should not move in use, should have a flat, level surface, be wide enough to take a metre-wide fabric, and be at a convenient working height.

If the intention is to print or screen a number of long lengths or large hangings, the table should be as long and heavy as space will allow. This will save much moving of the fabric during printing.

Figure 2.2. Covering the printing table (section)

The aim is to have as rigid a table as possible with a level top that still has a little 'give' during printing.

The table frame can be constructed from Dexion, Speed-frame, Handy Angle, or similar materials, or from 50 mm (2 in) square softwood with glued and pinned joints. The top should be screwed or bolted to this frame, with the heads countersunk and filled so as to give a completely smooth, level top.

A sheet of blockboard, chipboard, plywood, Contiplas, or a similar board in a convenient size – such as 125 cm (4 ft) square or 180 cm (6 ft) by 125 cm (4 ft) – by 12 mm (½ in) or 25 mm (1 in) in thickness, will make an excellent top.

The top will require one or two layers, without mends or joins, of blanket, carpet underlay, or 8mm (¼in) foam sheeting to act as padding. This in turn should be covered with plastic or rubber waterproof sheeting. (Marley heavy quality film is excellent. 'American cloth' will not stand up to heavy wear.) The layers will require fastening to the top. This can be done by tacking along the table edges (not the top), making sure that each layer is stretched as tightly as possible and no bumps or folds have been left to interfere with even printing. Alternatively, the covering can be fixed by stretching and fastening it down with strips of lath all round along or underneath the edges of the tabletop (*Figure 2.2*).

Where a table can be reserved for printing, a useful luxury is a simple cover to put over the printing surface when it is not in use. Other work can then be done on this cover without the risk of damaging the printing area.

Other most useful items are a side bench, shelf, or trolley, on which to place or mix dyes, equipment, etc., as well as an ironing board or table, storage cupboards (to hold dye jars and chemicals), and a clothes-horse or drier.

Basic equipment

Clean, screw-topped glass jars in which to store dyes and chemicals. It is advisable to keep jars of dye in a cool, dark cupboard. Avoid plastic pots since some pigment colours will dissolve plastic.

Large plastic buckets, bowls, pans and/or jars in which to mix dyes and to use as dyebaths for cold dyes. Hot dyes will require saucepans or dyebaths to withstand heat.

Large and small spoons, a long-bladed dinner knife, scissors, craft knife, ruler or metal tape, stapler, clear adhesive tape, greaseproof paper, a few medium and large plastic bags, clothespegs.

A steam iron, a small portable convector heater or a hairdryer.

Assorted paintbrushes, 12mm (½in) and 25mm (1in) varnish brushes, mixing sticks.

Rubber gloves, overall or apron, clean rag, sponge, dry clean newspaper.

3

Dyes and chemicals

Dyes

Almost any substance will stain to a greater or lesser degree;
many will be partially retained by fibres after washing or
exposure to light. Relatively few will form firm bonds between dye and fibre and become fast to light, able to
withstand washing or even boiling, resistant to atmospheric
or other contamination, and resistant to rubbing or a tendency to later bleeding (running or marking-off of colour), and
yet be easy to apply and fix.

There are two forms of colouring that have been used in
textile decoration since earliest times. There is the true
dyestuff, which unites with the fibre and leaves it with its
natural look and handle. There is also the pigment colour,
really a form of paint, which coats the fibre, often hiding the
natural qualities of fine fabrics.

Natural dyes have almost vanished, except for those still
available for use by the individual hand-craftsman, and a
large number of the earlier chemical dyes, particularly those
developed for natural fibres, are now rarely used. Even so,
some 8000 different dyestuffs are still in use in most of the
major countries of the world.

The following pages briefly describe those dyes most
useful and available to the craftsman-dyer. Recipes for many
of these dyes will be found in Chapter 12, suppliers' names
and addresses in Appendix 1, and a selected list of books on
dyeing in Appendix 2.

Natural dyes

From the wealth of imported natural dyes once available, about two dozen can still be purchased. Of course, it is possible to use many plants and vegetables to obtain dyes. Some of the most useful include the substantive dyes: that is, ones that are fast but do not require mordants, such as lichen and walnuts. As well, there are the adjective dyes that do require mordants to make them fast, including elderberries, onionskins, and weld.

Imported natural dyes based on plant or vegetable sources include indigo, obtained from the plant *Indigofera tinctoria* and giving a deep blue colour. It is one of the most ancient dyes known. Madder, from the roots of the plant *Rubia tinctorum*, yields a rich red colour; it is another very ancient dyestuff. Logwood, from the Central American tree *Haematoxylon campechianum*, produces purple on wool, blue and black on cotton, violet and black on silk. Cutch, from the Indian tree *Acacia catechu*, gives a rich dark brown colour. Young or zante fustic, from the powdered wood of the shrub *Rhus cotinus*, gives yellows to dark olive. Old fustic, from the wood of a tropical American tree *Chlorophora tinctoria*, gives gold to yellow colours.

Dyes based on animal sources include cochineal, obtained from the dried bodies of the insect *Coccus cacti* and providing a rich red dye.

These dyes give varying shades, tones, or colours according to the type of mordant used.

They are particularly useful in the tie-and-dye and wax or starch resist techniques. Recipes for a number of natural dyes will be found in the *Beginner's Guide to Spinning* in this series.

Direct dyes

These are among the earliest manmade dyes that were developed in the late 19th century for dyeing cotton and other cellulosic fibres. Most are reasonably fast to light or to washing, few are fast to both.

Acid dyes

These dyes are usually classed with the direct dyes, but they are of special use in the dyeing or, when suitably thickened, in the printing of wool and natural silk. They are easy to use, require only short dyeing times for many of the wide range of colours, and are relatively cheap. A small palette will give a large number of most attractive mixtures.

Vat dyes

The insoluble vat dyes provide some of the fastest dyes known, and many are still in use. As far as most amateur fabric printers are concerned, the special steam treatment they require is outside their scope.

For the dyer and the worker in wax or starch batik, the most useful is natural (or synthetic) indigo, one of the most important and prized dyes of history. Used mainly on cellulosic fibres, it will also dye wool and silk. The dyeing takes place in two stages.

As the dye is insoluble in water and so unable to directly dye the fibre, dyers utilise the ability of indigo to assume a 'leuco' form when treated with chemical reducing agents. In the first stage, the fabric is immersed in a vat, where it absorbs the dye in its leuco form. In the second stage, which is most exciting to watch, the fabric is gently withdrawn from the vat and exposed to the air. As it emerges, the oxygen in the air regenerates the original colour as an insoluble precipitate trapped within the fibre. The change in the fabric colour, from a dull yellow in the vat, through green, to a rich blue, after a few seconds in the air, is most dramatic.

Soluble vat dyes

Vat dyes are not particularly stable in the reduced or leuco stage. In the 1920s, a stable salt of leuco-indigo was discovered, and this started the development of a range of stable compounds of other vat dyes.

These soluble vat dyes are soluble in water or weak alkaline solutions and are applied in an ordinary hot or cold dyebath, or, with thickening, are used for printing without elaborate apparatus. They will dye cotton, silk, and wool. They are very fast.

Mordant (adjective) dyes

The most used of this class of dyes is an ancient one, madder, which yields a rich crimson from its roots. It will dye wool and silk, and, with the addition of alum, cotton.

The name originated in the necessity to apply this form of dye in the presence of a mordant, a chemical that precipitates the dye as an insoluble 'lake' within the fibre. Different mordants applied with the dye will produce different shades or even colours.

A sub-group called 'chrome colours' is particularly suitable for printing by the craftsman but not for dyeing.

Basic dyes

The term 'basic' refers only to the chemical nature of this group of dyes. These are exceedingly bright colours, but unfortunately they have very poor fastness to both washing and light. They will dye or, when thickened, print silk and wool. For cotton, a mordant is necessary.

They are useful for stage costumes, hangings, and interior display material.

Reactive dyes

Developed in the 1950s on a new chemical principle, reactive dyes form a stable and direct chemical linkage with cellulosic fibres to produce brilliant colours with maximum all-round fastness. There are a number eminently suitable for cold dyeing and for wax and starch batik, as well as for block and screen printing when thickened.

The ICI range of Procion M dyes is easy to use and fix. They are particularly good on mercerised cotton, good on cotton-satin, cotton, and viscose rayon. They give slightly paler shades on linen, natural silk, and chlorinated wool.

Other ranges of reactive dyes have been created, such as Procion H and Supra dyes (ICI), Cibacron and Reactone (Ciba-Geigy), Levafix (Bayer), Drimarene (Sandoz), and Remazol (Hoechst). All these require some form of steam treatment.

It is the more reactive Procion M range that is most useful to the craft dyer and printer. Because they possess such excellent power of penetration, care must be taken if they are used for tie-and-dye. Unless colours are very thoroughly washed out after fixation, there is a tendency for some to 'bleed'.

Procion dyes are not suitable for pad painting with starchy vegetables such as potatoes, since starch prevents Procion from developing in the fabric. However, this can be utilised in an elementary form of discharge or resist printing to produce quite attractive textured prints on a plain-dyed ground.

Since these dyestuffs are exceptionally fast and will stain almost anything, it is essential to use rubber gloves, to have plenty of newspaper on the working area, to avoid scattering the dry powder, and to clear up as soon as possible with cold water.

Pigment dyes

These are based on organic colouring matter that is insoluble in water and has to be attached to the fibre by the use of resinous binders which are fixed ('cured' or made insoluble) by heat (e.g., by ironing or baking).

Since they coat the fibre instead of dyeing it, they are applicable to almost any fabric except those with a pile or whose fibres would be affected by the heat-fixing process.

They are especially suitable for screen, block, and pad printing, direct painting, starch resist, and such minor techniques as stippling, stencilling, and combing.

Modern pigment colours leave the fabric far less stiff than the earlier forms, although care must be taken not to apply the colour too thickly to fine materials. The colour range is wide and all are intermixable within each particular range. Some suppliers include opaque white for printing or painting on dark grounds, as well as metallic and fluorescent colours. They are readily available in small and large packagings. An added advantage for beginners is that these colours are cleaned up with cold water.

Inks

Inks are a very useful form of pigment colour which has been mixed with oils. Best purchased in tubes, they are excellent, when used straight from the tube, for wood and lino block printing of articles that will remain flat in use, such as placemats. (This limitation is necessary as inks, when dry, tend to stiffen the fabric.) Blocks do not need to be flocked (see Chapter 8).

For pad printing, inks should be thinned with thinning oil, and there is no appreciable stiffening of the fabric. Blocks need to be flocked (explained in Chapter 8).

A reducing medium is available to obtain pale colours without the chalkiness that results if white is used. When mixing pale colours, always start with reducing medium, white, or the lightest colour, adding deeper tones last. It requires only a small amount of black, for example, to turn several times the same quantity of white into a dark grey.

When completely dry, ink-printed fabrics have good fastness to light and washing. Ironing on the reverse side when dry will improve handle.

Clean up with paraffin, not water.

Dyes for the beginner

The dyes listed in the table on pp. 12–13 are the easiest for the amateur to obtain and use. The beginner will be well advised to find out which are obtainable locally or from one supplier and stay with that group of dyes and colours, at least while experimenting. One could, for instance, use only Dylon Cold, Ultra-Batik, Multi-Purpose Dyes, and Color-Fun colours for all the techniques given in Chapters 5 to 10.

When using Dylon Multi-Purpose and Cold Dyes, it is not necessary to mix up a whole tin of dye at once. For small samples, tip out a small amount of dye into a bowl, then seal up the tin immediately with adhesive tape. Each tin contains approximately two level teaspoons of dye.

By choosing a very limited range of colours to start with (e.g., a good yellow, red, and blue, possibly black) many colours can be achieved by mixing. Dissolve some of the yellow, red, and blue in separate bowls, then experiment with mixing the three colours in other bowls so as to vary the range. The addition of a very little black will darken or change

Dyes, fabrics and suitable techniques for the beginner

Fabric	Dylon Cold	Dylon Multi-Purpose or Liquid	Dylon Ultra	Inks[1]	Fixer type[2]	Natural	Pigment colours[3]	Procion M
Acetate rayon		*o		*+	*		*+	
Acrilan				*+			*+	
Banlon		*o		*+			*+	
Bri-nylon		*o		*+			*+	
Canvas	*			*+		*	*+	
Cashmere			*	*+			*+	
Cashmilon				*+	*		*+	
Celon		*o	*	*+			*+	
Cotton	*o	*o		*+		*o	*+	
Sarille	*			*+			*+	*
Silk	*o	*o	*	*+		*o	*+	*
Sisal	*		*	*+		*	*+	
Spanzelle		*o					+	
Tendrelle (tights)		*o		*+			*+	
Tergal		*		*+			*+	
Terienka		*		*+			*+	
Terlinga		*		*+			*+	
Terylene		*		*+			*+	

	Batik	Block	Direct brush painting	Discharge (of non-fast colours)	Pad or scrap	Screen	Stencil or stipple	Tie-and-dye
Courtelle		*	*		*	*		*
Crimplene	**	*	*		*	*		+ *
Dacron	**	*	*		*	*		+ *
Dicel	**	*	*		*	*		* +
Diolen	**	*	*		*	*		* +
Dralon		*	*		*	*		*
Enkalon	*o	*				*		
Fibreglass	*							
Jute	*	*	*		*	*		**
Helanca	*o	*	*		*	*		+ *
Hemp	*	*	*		*	*		*
Leacril	*o	*	*		*	*		+ *
Linen	*o	*	*	*o	*	*		*
Lycra		*	*	*	*	*		*
Neospun	*o	*	*		*	*		+
Nylon		*	*		*	*		*
Orlon	*o	*	*		*	*		+ *
Perlon	*o	*	*		*	*		+
Polyester/cotton	**	**	**	**o	*	**	*	**
P.V.C.	**	**	*			*		**
Trevira	**	**			+	**		+ *
Tricel	**	**			+	**		+ *
Vincel (non-pleat)	*	o	o		*	*	o	* +
Viscose	*o	o	o		*	*	o	* +
Wool	**	o	o	*	+	*	o	*

Suitable techniques

Key
* Suitable.
** Only medium shades obtainable.
o Suitable if thickened with Manutex or other gum for printing.
+ Suitable when thinned and used from a pad or brush.

Notes
1 Including Lawrence's Oil Fabric Inks, Arnold's Block Printing Ink, Reeves' Printing Inks.
2 Including Arnold's Dyesticks and Fabraprint, Fabricol, Reeves' Craft Dyes.
3 Including Accolite, Aquaprint, Aqua-Set, Dylon Color-Fun, Fabritint, Helizarin, Polyprint, Printex, Screen and Fabric Printing Colour, Screen Printing Colour, Texiscreen, Tintolite, Versatex.

13

a colour. If pale colours are wanted, it is possible to use a smaller amount of a deep-coloured dye; this is more economical than buying, for example, a pale blue and a deep blue dye.

Precautions and remedies

Always open tins or containers over newspaper. Dye powder is very fine, and can be easily spilt. Carefully screw up the top sheet of newspaper and throw it away after mixing dye, to prevent grains of dye from going astray.

Dyes will stain whatever and wherever they splash, so take care with floors, walls, clothing and skin. If accidentally splashed, wash dye off at once with plenty of clean, cold water. If it is splashed into the eyes, bathe them immediately with cold water and refer to a doctor at once. Keep a well-stocked first-aid box.

Wear an apron and rubber gloves, and mix dyes over newspaper. Use a clean, dry spoon for each dye or chemical. Replace lids, etc., on dyes and chemicals immediately after use.

Label any left-over dye or gum. Most mixed pigment dyes will keep for at least a few days in screw-topped glass jars in a cool place. Mixed Dylon Cold, Procion, and other reactive dyes will not keep for longer than an hour or so.

Always wash up bowls, brushes, equipment, etc., immediately after use. Dyes allowed to dry in brushes, screens, blocks, etc., are often impossible to remove. Methylated spirits may help to dissolve hardened dye.

Work in a well ventilated room and avoid smoking or naked flames when using dyes containing inflammable solvents (e.g., certain pigment dyes).

If a dye or pigment colour is accidentally dropped on a fabric, carefully remove at once any surplus with a clean spoon, blunt knife, blotting paper, or bunched-up rag. Avoid spreading the stain or rubbing it into the cloth. Keep the stain wet with a drop or two of cold water.

On a white fabric or one with a fast ground colour, the

stain can be removed or reduced with Dygon, depending on the fastness of the stain. Try a little Dygon on the back edge of the fabric before using it on the stain in order to test the fastness of the ground colour.

To apply Dygon, check first that the stain is still damp; if not, moisten it. Place a pad of clean white cloth underneath the stain and sprinkle a little Dygon over the stain. Gently rub it with an old soft toothbrush, then sponge the stain. Repeat if necessary. Avoid inhaling or using Dygon in a confined space.

An alternative method is to apply the Dygon mixed with a little cold water to the stain. Allow it to dry and then iron, using a steam iron, with the fabric between clean cloth or paper at a temperature suitable for the fabric. Finally, sponge the area treated.

Much more difficult stains to deal with are those from a non-dischargeable dye, or one which has dried and set in the fibre, or where the background colour is not very fast. If the stain will be hidden by further patterning or the design can be adapted to disguise it, then it is best left alone. Otherwise, do not attempt to deal with it until all processes have been completed, including fixation and the final ironing. The stain should then be masked with a white or appropriately coloured pigment (such as Color-Fun, Printex, or Polyprint). This is best applied with a soft stencil brush in a light powdering motion and as thinly as possible.

Spots of wax or grease can be removed by first dropping a little cold water on the unwanted wax in order to solidify it and stop it penetrating. Next, scrape off as much wax as possible with a blunt knife. Place clean blotting paper below and above, and iron. The last traces can be removed with a proprietary grease remover.

It is not advisable to use household bleaches. Many contain chlorine, which adversely affects silk, wool, and nylon, and concentrated bleach will rot cotton, linen, and rayon.

Do not use oxalic acid on silk or wool, acetone or nail-varnish remover on acetate rayon or Tricel, or grease solvents on plastics.

Thickeners

By itself, a dye, when mixed with water, is too thin to use for printing from a pad, or with a block or screen, or when painting directly on to a fabric (but not for tie-and-dye, wax batik, or starch resist). A bland thickening agent, usually a starch or gum, is used to thicken the dye mixture to a consistency suitable for printing or painting. It should be soluble in water, not clog the screen or the surface of a block, and be easily removable from the fabric after fixation and during washing-off.

There are a number of thickeners available, but the easiest to mix, use, and store are those based on sodium alginate, manufactured from seaweed, such as Manutex (G.B.) or Keltex (U.S.A.), which are supplied in powder form. (For recipes see Chapter 12.) They are suitable for all dyestuffs mentioned in this chapter. They are essential for all forms of reactive dyes, including Procion, and can be used for thickening pigment colours if this is necessary.

Suitability of dyes and thickeners

	Acid	Basic	Direct	Dylon Cold	Dylon Multi-Purpose	Dylon Ultra	Fixer type	Natural	Pigment	Procion M	Soluble vat
British gum	x	x	x		x			x			
Gum arabic / Gum senegal	x	x			x		x	x			x
Nafka crystal gum	x		x		x						
Gum dragon / Gum tragacanth	x	x	x		x		x				
Sodium alginate (Manutex/Keltex)	x		x	x	x	x	x		x	x	x
Starch/tragacanth	x	x	x		x						

Other gums used by textile printers include the following.

British gum is a starch-based thickener which is difficult to remove from fabric after fixation; it is used mainly by block printers, as it is a rather sticky paste with a high solid content. Gum arabic, gum senegal, gum tragacanth, and gum dragon are all useful gums, very laborious to mix but quite easily washed out after fixation. Mixtures of laundry starch and gum tragacanth are are also used. Nafka gum, most useful for direct and acid dyestuffs and also in discharge printing, is simple to mix and easy to wash out. It is particularly good for printing on silk.

The beginner will undoubtedly find Manutex or Keltex the best thickeners for normal use, and, when mixed, they will keep for several weeks.

Chemicals

Some dyestuffs need to be used in combination with certain chemicals; details will be found in Chapter 12. The following table lists those which have common names.

Common name	Chemical name
Washing soda	Sodium carbonate
Common salt	Sodium chloride
Glauber's salt	Sodium sulphate
Potash	Anhydrous potassium carbonate
Soda ash	Anhydrous sodium carbonate

Always keep chemicals under lock and key since many are poisonous or will burn or stain.

Protecting finished work

It is often useful to protect such finished work as hangings and cushion covers. There are several aerosol sprays on the market which will give a dirt and water repellent finish to fabrics. It is advisable to try such a spray on a piece of fabric printed with the same dyes as on the finished article; test pieces on scrap fabric are suitable. If the colours are fast, the spray can be used as directed on the container. It will not change the colour, appearance, or handle of the fabric. Scotchguard is highly recommended, others include Fabsil and Nev.

Other aerosol sprays, such as 103 Letraset Matt (G.B.) and Getzol Type 'C' Matte Lacquer (U.S.A.), are useful to protect work against damage by sunlight, mildew, high humidity and moisture, and to eliminate glare or uneven shine. Experiment on test prints or dyeings.

Use aerosol sprays only in well ventilated spaces away from heat or open flame. Avoid prolonged contact with skin or eyes, and keep them out of reach of children.

Records, recipes and samples

A problem encountered by many dyers and printers is how to repeat an exact match of a dye colour, a recipe for a resist or paste, or a particular effect which may originally have been obtained by chance.

This can be overcome by keeping a record, preferably in looseleaf form. It should include dye recipes with exact quantities and proportions of dye and chemicals used, plus any individual variation, method of application, length of time, and method of fixation, together with dyed and/or printed fabric samples of colours used. These notes and samples will not only form an interesting diary but will also avoid endless repetition and experimenting when planning future work.

A similar collection of fabric samples, showing how a particular fabric reacted to a particular dye, or the effect of experiments in tie-dyeing or batik on differing materials, etc., will form a useful pattern and reference book (though it is not possible to exactly reproduce a tie-dyed or batik effect).

The beginner will accumulate a large number of samples, trial or test pieces, and discarded cuttings of fabrics.

Although many are best retained, there will be others not required. With a little ingenuity, most of these can be put to good use, in conjunction with pieces of plain, white, coloured, textured, or patterned fabric, to make cushion covers, aprons, wall hangings, cot covers, tea-cosies, patchwork, etc.

Smaller pieces can be used for making needle cases, pincushions, bookmarkers, herb or lavender sachets, egg cosies, finger puppets, dolls' clothes, dollshouse furnishings, glove or other puppets, etc. (Plate 1).

4

Fabrics and fabric preparation

Fabrics

There are two main classes of fabric. The oldest, consisting of those woven from natural fibres, contains two sub-classes. One includes fibres derived from animal sources; the most important are wool and natural silk, but there are also many fur and hair fibres, such as alpaca, camel, cashmere, hog, llama, mohair, and vicuna.

The other group consists of those woven from fibres obtained from vegetable sources. Here the most important are cotton, flax (linen), and jute. The many others include those of the bast varieties (made from inner tree barks) hemp, kapok, raffia, ramie, sisal, straw, etc.

The second class of fabric is comprised by those constructed from manmade fibres. Again there are two sub-classes. In one, the fibres are a modified form of a natural fibre, such as viscose rayon, which is based on cellulose obtained either from cotton linters or, as is more common nowadays, from woodpulp.

In the other are the large ranges of entirely manmade fibres, including polyesters (Crimplene, Dacron, Diolen, Tergal, Terlinga, Terylene, etc.), acrylics (Acrilan, Cashmilon, Courtelle, Dralon, Leacril, Orlon, etc.), nylons/polyamides (Banlon, Bri-nylon, Celon, Enkalon, Perlon, etc.).

Additionally there are a number of miscellaneous fibres, including those made from minerals, the most important of which is asbestos. Others of more specialised use are spun glass, slag wool, tinsel threads, and the various threads obtained from gold, silver, copper, and alloys.

Mixtures, or unions, of the various classes, such as polyester/cotton, Terylene/wool, silk/wool, cotton/linen and the like, attempt to exploit the best qualities of each component fibre. However, they present problems to the textile dyer and printer, since different dyes have different natural preferences or affinities for particular types of fibre.

For the beginner, certain of the above are very difficult to dye or print, either because the fibre repels the dye used or because the fibre demands advanced techniques beyond the scope and facilities of the amateur.

Identification

When a length of material does not possess a label of washing instructions which may help to determine the particular fibre or fibres used, or the supplier of the fabric is unable to help, there is an easy method of broadly identifying a fibre. This is by burning. To do this, stand a nightlight or candle in a basin of water on a baking tray or piece of metal cooking foil. Use tweezers or pliers to hold a thread of fabric in the flame, and notice the way it burns and the smell it gives off.

Wool or silk will give a smell of burning feathers, and although the fibre will continue to char as long as it is held in the flame, it will go out as soon as it is removed from it and form a black bead at the end. With wool, this ash is hard; with silk it is friable. (Do not touch the bead until it is cold.)

Cotton, linen, and viscose rayon fibres burn with a smell of charred paper, carry on burning after removal from the flame, and do not form a bead.

Polyester (e.g. Dacron) burns slowly and melts. A hard black or brown bead forms. A chemical smell is given off.

Acetate rayon (usually a shiny fabric) forms a black bead which shrinks from the flame and can be crushed.

Nylon and Terylene also shrink from the flame and give a hard, uncrushable bead. Nylon smells of celery; Terylene has an aromatic smell.

The identification of the entirely manmade fibres is most complex, apart from their tendency to soften and melt when heated. Testing kits of chemical stains are available for this purpose.

Testing
To test the compatibility of a dye with a particular fibre, the simplest method is to wash a sample piece of the fabric as thoroughly as possible to remove any dressing applied during manufacture. Then apply the chosen dye or pigment, following all the instructions for that dye and the chosen process. After dyeing or printing and fixing, cut the sample piece in half. Place one half on one side and finish the other half according to the instructions (washing, ironing, etc.). It is then possible to compare the fastness of the dye or pigment to washing and rubbing.

To test light-fastness, cut the second (washed) half, in halves. Tape one half on to the inside of a window, if possible facing south and with the design or face-side facing outwards. Place the first (unwashed) half and the washed quarter away from light. After a week of exposure, compare the three pieces.

It is, in the end, better to fully check a fabric in this manner than to waste a whole piece or length of fabric.

Of course, if fabrics are prepared for printing and fully identified by the supplier, as are many supplied in short lengths by Whaleys of Bradford, there should be no problems.

Certain fabrics are very difficult to dye or print at home. These include all the acrylics previously listed, pleated Tricel, anything with a special finish (drip-dry, proofed in any way, shrink resistant, with fillers, etc.), cashmere, angora, spunglass or glass fibre fabric, mohair, skins, felt, plastic sponge cloth, and anything which has a bonded lining or interlining or a foam or plastic backing. Special paint-on dyes are available for suede and leathers.

This still leaves most of the important natural fibres as very suitable for the beginner in dyeing and printing. Two treatments applied to cotton are mercerisation and a satin finish.

These often improve the appearance of the finished work, particularly when reactive dyes have been employed.

Fabric preparation

Except for fabrics supplied ready for dyeing or printing, it is essential that fabrics are very well washed before dyeing or printing to remove all dressings, impurities, dirt, or stains. Many dressings are resin based and so very resistant to washing. Unless you are completely certain that the fabric you wish to use is free of impurities and dressings, you must remove them or they may repel the dyes, preventing them from reaching the fibres. This will give patchy prints, or the dye will wash or wear off in use.

The following methods will help to remove some finishes – i.e., to 'scour' the fabric. They are effective for size (added to the yarn before weaving); filler (added to the woven cloth to improve the feel, thickness, or weight, starch being easier to remove than a resin based filler); finish (drip-dry, non-woven, mini-care, sanforised, crease resistant, pre-shrunk, etc., which are all very difficult to remove).

First soak all fabrics, preferably overnight, in cold water.

Cotton and linen Boil for half an hour in water containing a little soapless detergent (Stergene, Lissapol, or Teepol in G.B.; Duponal or Synthrapol in the U.S.A.). Do not use a detergent containing a 'whitener' or 'bluer', etc.

Silk Nearly boil (be certain not to boil or you will spoil the feel and appearance of the silk) for one hour in a weak solution of liquid detergent. This is termed 'de-gumming'. Do not twist or wring the silk, but squeeze it out very gently.

Wool Wash gently for half an hour in a very weak solution, hand-hot (50°C [120°F]) only, of Stergene, etc., in water. Do not rub or stir in case the wool felts or hardens.

Nylon and Terylene Soak in a weak solution of Stergene, etc., and water for half an hour.

Rayon, viscose Boil for half an hour in a weak solution of Stergene and water.

Acetate Soak for half an hour in a weak solution of Stergene, etc., water, and a few drops of ammonia. (Take care – ammonia is dangerous.)

After scouring, all fabrics must be thoroughly rinsed in clean, cold water, dried, and ironed.

The physical structure of the fabric will affect not only the dye used, but twilled, heavily corded or ribbed cloths, and those with diagonal weaves or textures will affect batik, and block and screen printed designs. Heavy, thick fabrics give very strong, bold effects to tie-and-dye, whereas fine silk or cambric make intricate detail possible. Brushed and pile cloths will absorb more dye than plain cloth. A very different quality is apparent when a dye is used on fabrics woven from slub, crepe, or textured yarns from that given when a plain weave is used. Old and well-worn sheeting will tend to give a dull, worn appearance to any dyeing or printing used on it.

Many non-woven or bonded fabrics, particularly interlining fabrics, are suitable for hangings and panels printed with pigment colours.

Fabrics supplied as ready to dye or print will save much trouble and give the best results. Certain firms, particularly Whaleys of Bradford, supply short and long lengths of such fabrics, including silks, mercerised cottons, light and heavy cottons and linens, cotton satins, and woollens, as well as some unbleached (loomstate) fabrics. Other suppliers will be found in Appendix 1.

5

Tie-and-dye

For centuries, the craft of tie-and-dye was widespread in all parts of the world except Oceania and Australia. It was particularly developed in the great silk regions of India, China, and Japan, as well as in West Africa and parts of Central America.

Until the discovery of synthetic dyestuffs, the colours used were natural ones, such as the wonderful blue of indigo, the rich browns and reds of walnut, madder, and cochineal, and colours from lichens, including the deep purple of cudbear. Many of these are still obtainable, some from dealers and others by collecting in the countryside. Their preparation is, of course, much more laborious than the use of easily applied dyes such as Dylon Multi-Purpose Dyes and the very fast Dylon Cold Water Dyes, but they have helped to create a marked resurgence of interest in the craft. This is mainly due to the very original results obtainable, even by beginners, since the basic techniques of tie-and-dye are relatively simple, requiring the minimum of apparatus to create individual patterns. More complicated patterns can be developed as experience widens.

The basic principle of tie-and-dye is the same as that of batik, in that dye is prevented from reaching parts of the fabric. But whereas in batik, starch paste or wax is used as a 'resist', in tie-and-dye, the fabric is either knotted, or folded and tied up with thread, string, or raffia. When stitched with thread, which is pulled up very tightly and fastened before dyeing, the method is called 'tritik'.

The tied-up parts retain the original colour of the fabric. Further tying will 'resist' additional colours protecting areas of the first colour. Some of the original ties may be undone to allow a second colour to 'take' on the undyed areas after the first dyeing. It is the combination of these simple methods, together with careful planning of the final design and the use of colours, which produces the elaborate patterns shown in *Plate 2*.

Materials and equipment

Dylon Multi-Purpose Fabric Dyes and Dylon Liquid Dyes are very suitable for tie-and-dye techniques. Silk and wool require special treatment if they are to retain their soft, natural feel, which is easily affected by boiling or by harsh chemicals.

With fine and medium-weight fabrics, tying can be done with white or natural thread, fine string, or raffia. For heavier fabrics, it is advisable to use string and raffia (not plastic or coloured). In more advanced work, a variety of objects can be tied into the fabric.

For Dylon Multi-Purpose Fabric Dyes, a saucepan is necessary as they need to be heated. For Dylon Cold Water Dyes, Procion M, or other reactive dyes, small articles can be dyed in jamjars, or plastic or glass basins. Larger articles can be dyed in plastic washing-up bowls or plastic buckets. Wide-based bowls are safer than narrow-based ones.

A sink, kettle, saucepan, water, spoons, stirring sticks, rag, newspaper, a small pair of thin-bladed scissors, an apron, rubber gloves, and some form of table covering will be necessary, and a clothes-horse is useful for drying.

If your water supply is hard, add a small amount of Calgon; this will soften the water and improve it for dyeing.

Colour

It is very important to consider the use of colour when planning a piece of work. Two tones of a colour (e.g., pale blue and deep blue) require different planning from two colours (e.g., pink and blue).

In the first case, decide which part of the fabric is to be left as the background colour (white if you are using a white fabric) and bind and tie this area. Dye in pale blue. Leave the binding on the fabric, rinse thoroughly, and squeeze out. Add further binding to protect some of the pale-blue areas. Now dye in deep blue. After rinsing, etc., carefully cut the ties and remove the bindings. The result should be a pattern of white, pale blue, and deep blue.

In the second case, if blue and pink are used, it is possible to achieve three colours – blue, pink, and purple – plus the white ground. Decide on the areas to be left white and pink in the finished pattern, then tie up both these areas. Dye the fabric in blue dye, rinse, and squeeze out. Leave the binding on in the areas to be white. Tie up some of the area now dyed blue. Carefully remove the binding from the areas to be pink. As these have been protected from the blue dye, they are at present white and will pick up a true pink clearly. Where blue is still exposed, the pink will mix with it to produce purple. Dye in the pink dye, rinse, squeeze out, then carefully remove the bindings.

First experiments

The beginner is advised to experiment with basic methods before planning more advanced work.

For these first experiments, some pieces of thin, white cotton fabric, such as old handkerchiefs, pieces of old sheets, pillowcases, calico, muslin, poplin or cambric, will be needed.

It is not possible to say exactly how tight a tying or binding thread should be tied; the tighter it is, the more it will resist the dye. By experimenting, the beginner will soon discover how tight the binding must be.

When tying a long section of fabric (e.g., where areas are reserved for several future colours, or when protecting dyed areas before dyeing in a final dark colour), the beginner can easily fall into the trap shown in *Figure 5.1a*. Here the string, raffia, or thread is started at the top and bound round until the required area is covered. It will then be found that there is one end at the top and one at the base, so it is impossible to tie the two ends together.

To overcome this problem, leave one loose end of string at the base, take the string to the top of the area, and, holding it in place between a thumb and finger, use the other hand to bind the fabric. When the binding is complete, the first end will be there to be tied to the second end (*Figure 5.1b*).

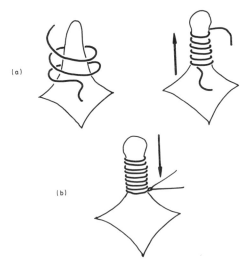

Figure 5.1. A method of tying for tie-and-dye. (a) Incorrect. (b) Correct

Once techniques have been chosen and a finished piece of work decided on (e.g., a cushion cover), it is advisable to do samples with the chosen fabric and dye. Keep all samples for future use as described in Chapter 3.

When doing initial experiments, don't be discouraged if, for example, ties have been made too loosely and the resulting patterns are disappointing. Tie up the fabric again, even in a different pattern, and redye it in a deeper colour.

If two colours are being used, make sure the resulting mixture of the two will be a good colour: e.g., pink plus orange will give red where the two colours mix.

If two shades of one colour are being used, it is advisable to use the pale shade first.

If a single colour is used, a deep shade will produce more interesting effects than a pale shade.

For finished pieces, it is advisable to use fabric prepared for dyeing either when purchased or by scouring. The simplest way of scouring cotton and linen is to soak the fabric overnight in a mild soda bath and wash thoroughly next day in very hot water and soda. Rinse very well. Cotton and linen (but not silk or wool) can be boiled if required. Good rinsing is essential (see also Chapter 4).

Dylon Multi-Purpose Fabric Dyes are suggested for first experiments, as, although they require heating, they are simple to use and will give the keen beginner a quicker result than Dylon Cold Water or Procion M Dyes. However, results on old cloth will not be as good as on new cloth, so don't be discouraged if colours seem 'chalky'. At this stage, it is important to master techniques and get used to using dyes.

Always hand-wash hand printed or dyed articles.

Knotting

Of the several basic ties, the easiest is knotting. For this you will need a large piece of thin, white cloth about 60 cm (24 in) square. Pleat this like a concertina, then knot it once at each

Figure 5.2. Knotting dry pleated fabric for tie-and-dye

Figure 5.3. Knotting centre and all four corners of a piece of damp fabric

Figure 5.4. Knotting centre and two opposite corners of dry fabric

end (*Figure 5.2*). Take a second piece of cloth, wet it in cold water, and squeeze it out; hold it up by the centre with one hand and use the other hand to smooth the cloth down so that it hangs in even folds. Knot it just under the centre and once at each corner (*Figure 5.3*). Take a third piece of cloth, do not wet it, but knot it like the second piece but with only two corners knotted (*Figure 5.4*).

Prepare the dye, following the makers' instructions (see Chapter 12). Wet the three pieces of tied fabric, squeeze them out, place them in the dyebath, and dye according to instructions.

Remove the fabric from the dye, rinse it thoroughly in cold water, squeeze it out and leave it until partly dry.

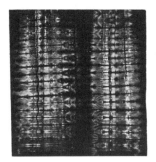

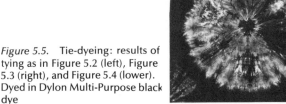

Figure 5.5. Tie-dyeing: results of tying as in Figure 5.2 (left), Figure 5.3 (right), and Figure 5.4 (lower). Dyed in Dylon Multi-Purpose black dye

Undo the knots, then iron the samples flat, using an iron setting to suit the type of fabric. It is advisable to have a piece of old sheeting or cotton fabric on top of the ironing surface and to cover the dyed or printed sample with another piece when ironing. This prevents any loose dye from spoiling the ironing cloth or being picked up on the iron and transferred.

Compare the spread of the dye in fabrics tied wet or dry, as well as the different results of knotting and pleating (*Figure 5.5*).

Marbling
This is an effective method of producing an overall texture. Crumple up a piece of fabric – either wet or dry – and tie it into a light ball (a pad of newspaper or a ball can be tied inside) and dye as before. After untying, the fabric can be recrumpled, tied, and dyed in a second colour (*Figure 5.6*).

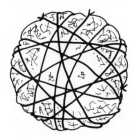

Figure 5.6. Binding to produce an all-over marbled texture

There are other ways of marbling. One is to crumple the fabric into a nylon stocking (or a leg of nylon tights), tie pieces of raffia or string around, and immerse it in the dye. Small pieces (handkerchiefs or scraps to be used for patchwork or trimmings, etc.) can be pushed into plastic hair rollers and tied in, or tied in a net or porous fabric and dyed. Use cold water dyes for the plastic roller technique.

Pegging and clipping
Fold the piece of fabric several times into a pad (*Figure 5.7*). Clip the edges together with paperclips or bulldog clips, or plastic or wooden clothes-pegs. Immerse in a cold dye (plastic clips distort in hot water).

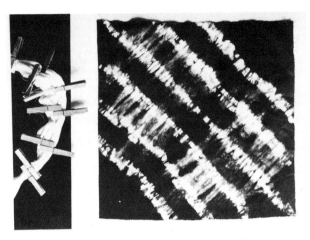

Figure 5.7. A 'pegged' fabric, before and after dyeing

After dyeing, blot the fabric between newspaper, remove the clips, and allow the fabric to dry before rinsing it in cold water. Metal clips will tend to rust if left wet for too long.

Binding-in
As has already been mentioned, many objects such as old tennis balls, corks, cotton reels, pebbles, dried pulses, small pieces of wood and wooden shapes can be tied into the fabric, as shown in *Figure 5.8a*. These will give a wide variety of spot shapes, depending on the article inserted.

This technique is sometimes known as 'clump tying', from the little bunches or clumps of fabric formed as the beads, etc., are bound in. It is widely used in West Africa, where very large rectangular cloths are elaborately decorated. In this country, it is most suitable for bedspreads, tablecloths, curtains, dividers, large shawls, and planned garments. For clothing, the design must be linked with the dress pattern to be used.

Several different objects can be tied into any one piece of fabric, but always start from the centre of the fabric and work outwards, leaving enough space between each tie to wrap the fabric around other objects.

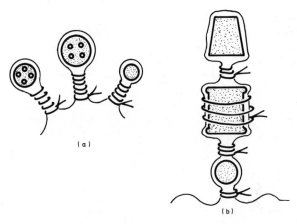

Figure 5.8. Tying-in objects, using (a) one or (b) several ties

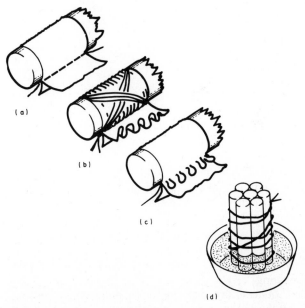

Figure 5.9. Gathered-in and bound ties. (a) Fabric wrapped round wood and tied (b) or stitched (c) with thread. (d) Dyeing a border

33

Once you have started to tie the fabric, it will become distorted, so before starting it is advisable to mark the centre of each tie with a small pencil dot.

Several objects can be tied one above the other, as in *Figure 5.8b*. Large objects can have further ties around them as well as those binding them in.

A development of binding-in is shown in *Figure 5.9*. The fabric is wrapped around a piece or pieces of circular or square wood (*a*). It is then tightly gathered at one end and trapped with very tight diagonal ties (*b*), or by inserting threads and pulling up (*c*). The rod or rods and the fabric are stood in a cold dye (*d*) to give a border pattern.

Ties with threads
A further piece of fabric is creased as shown by the dotted lines in *Figure 5.10a*. The ties at the points marked with a star are made with about six turns of thread up and down and knotted as in *Figure 5.10b*. At the centre of the fabric, an old

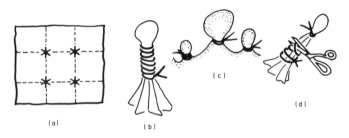

Figure 5.10. Tying with threads. (a) Marking positions of ties. (b) Tying. (c) Use of tennis ball at centre of fabric. (d) Cutting the ties

tennis ball is inserted, and a tie is made, fairly tightly, immediately underneath the ball with raffia or string. A space should be left before tying again, lower down (*c*) using coarse string.

Wet, squeeze, dye, part-dry, undo, and iron, as before.

To cut the ties, use small, thin-bladed scissors as in *Figure 5.10d*. It is very important not to cut the fabric itself when

Figure 5.11. Pleating and tying, before (bottom right) and after dyeing

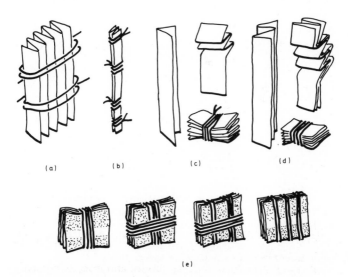

(a)   (b)   (c)   (d)

(e)

Figure 5.12. Pleating and folding. (a) First ties. (b) Fabric retied after dyeing. (c), (d), (e) Other methods of tying

cutting the ties, so insert one blade of the scissors under a single thread and cut it; the remainder of the tie can then be easily unwound.

Making stripes and checks
To make stripes and checks (*Figure 5.11*), the fabric is pleated in length and tied around at regular or irregular intervals (*Figure 5.12a*). It is then dyed, untied in part, further ties are added, and the fabric is re-dyed as required (*Figure 5.12b*).

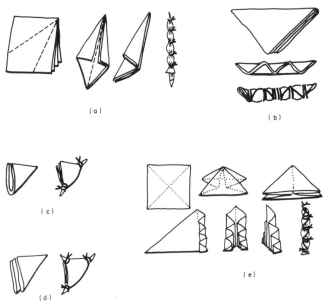

Figure 5.13. Square ties made by various methods. (a) Fold a large plain handkerchief into four; fold four corners to centre; fold down centre to leave corners exposed; tie, dye and rinse. Undo or retie as required. (b) Fold into four and on the diagonal to form a triangle; fold over twice; tie, dye, etc. (c) Fold into four and on the diagonal to form a triangle; tie two or three corners; dye, etc. (d) Fold with outside corners to each side; tie two or three corners; dye, etc. (e) Crease on dotted lines; tuck in sides; press flat; zig-zag-pleat one side to centre line, taking care to keep even, level sides; zig-zag other side; fold back to back; tie, dye, etc.

Another technique is to fold once and pleat down the fold (c). Dye, retie, redye as required.

The first fold can be made into two or more folds before pleating down (d), or the packet can also be tied across (e).

Square ties
Many varieties of patterns can be produced by folding a square of fabric in different ways. *Figure 5.13* shows a number of these.

Tie-and-dye for large areas

The examples already given cover the basic forms of binding in relatively small areas. Lengths and large pieces (beds-preads, hangings, etc.) require care and planning if the patterns are not to be distorted.

When pleating and tying across a wide piece of fabric (e.g., 90 cm [36 in]), it will be found after dyeing that the centre of the fabric is much paler than the outside pleats. This is because it is difficult for the dye to penetrate to the centre of the fabric. Where penetration is required, the pleats should be opened out as much as possible without distorting the bindings.

Large fabrics require very careful planning. For a pleated length, decide on the width of pleat. If this is to be, say, 25 mm (1 in), then make a row of pencil dots 50 mm (2 in) across the width of the fabric. Make further such rows of dots about 15 cm (6 in) apart down the complete length of the fabric. Pick up the first dots on the first two rows and take them across to meet the second dots. This will form a 25 mm (1 in) pleat as planned. Continue right across the fabric. Hold the pleats together with clothespegs until they have been tied with string or raffia where the pencil dots are. Continue down the length of fabric until pleating and tying are complete. It is sometimes easier to dampen the fabric before forming the pleats. Open out the pleats between the ties before dyeing.

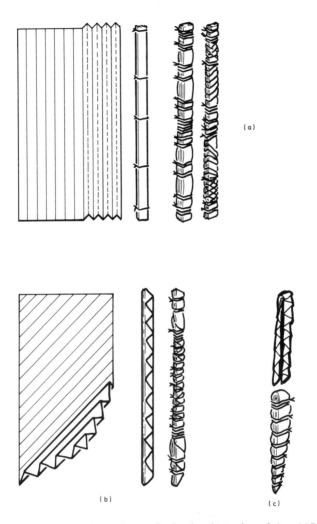

Figure 5.14. Alternative methods of making pleated ties. (a) Fabric pleated, loosely bound to hold it in place, and tied as required. (b) Fabric pleated on the diagonal, loosely bound, and tied as required. (c) The tied (or bound) pleated fabric can be folded over and then tied further

Pleated and rope ties

This method gives most interesting stripe patterns. *Figure 5.14* shows two different methods.

Because the pleating and tying protect much of the fabric, it is essential that there is not too much tying, that the ties are not too close together, and that, after tying, the pleats are opened out to allow the dye to penetrate as far as possible in the untied parts.

Tritik

Tritik, or stitched patterns (*Figure 5.15*), is a most effective method of patterning and is still widely practised in West Africa and parts of South and South-East Asia.

A strong thread such as button thread is sewn into the fabric with a running stitch (knotted at the loose end) and is then drawn up tightly and fastened off firmly with two or three over-stitches to keep the fabric drawn up securely. It is

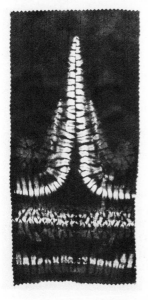

Figure 5.15. A tritik, or sewn resist, pattern (Patricia Robinson)

essential to fasten on and off securely; if the thread gives during the dyeing, the pattern will be spoilt.

There are many different ways of using this method to give spirals and animal, flower, bird, butterfly and other realistic shapes, as well as design forms.

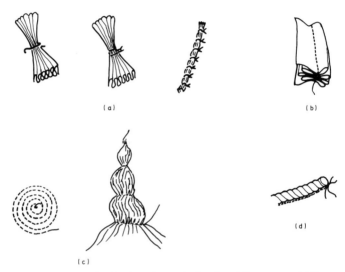

Figure 5.16. Methods of sewing and tying for tritik patterns. (a) Knot one end of a thread, pleat the fabric, and put a running thread through; return the running thread, pull up, and fasten off; repeat down the fabric as required; dye, etc. (b) Pleat the fabric and sew down, or across, or diagonally, or as a zig-zag; dye, etc. Sewing can be left or drawn up. (c) Sew and draw up a spiral; dye, etc. (d) Oversew the edge of a fold and draw up; dye, etc.

The basic stitch methods are shown in *Figure 5.16.* It is advisable to make two (or more) rows of stitching to ensure a better resist and give sharper definition. These should be at least 3 mm (⅛ in) to 6 mm (¼ in) apart.

The stitched fabric can be immersed in water and squeezed out before pulling up the threads; this will improve definition on most fabrics.

If a medium to heavy fabric is used, it may be necessary to sew with two thicknesses of thread.

If only one colour is to be used, and several rows of stitching have been made, the ends of the rows can be tied together.

If a radiating pattern has been planned, commence pulling up from the centre.

If several areas of pattern have been planned, complete all the sewing and leave the ends loose; complete all sewing before pulling up to avoid confusion when the fabric becomes distorted.

Take great care when cutting threads after dying and rinsing have been completed.

Discharge tying

An unusual technique is discharge tying, which gives the design in colour and the background in white or a pale shade.

The fabric is dyed with a dye which can be bleached out afterwards to white or a paler shade. The technique is not suitable for polyesters, acrylics, Tricel, materials with special finishes (e.g., drip-dry), or fast-dyed fabrics. Wool requires special treatment.

Dye the fabric according to makers' instructions. When it has been rinsed and dried, knot, tie, or sew by any of the methods already described, remembering that all exposed areas will be affected by the bleach solution.

Mix Dygon according to the makers' instructions or use a very mild solution of household bleach (one part bleach to six parts water). Too strong a solution will rot the fabric. Take care. Concentrated bleach is dangerous. Rinse very thoroughly in cold water after bleaching out. By varying the length of time in the bleach solution, many variations of texture and shading are possible.

Provided that all bleach has been removed from the fabric by thorough rinsing or washing, it is possible to tie or retie the fabric and dye it normally.

If commercially dyed fabrics are used, test a sample in a small amount of bleach solution to see if it is resistant to bleaching.

Further techniques

1. Interesting results can be achieved by mixing two or more different colours of the same class of dye in the same dyebath and dyeing the tied fabric in the mixture. It will be found that one colour will travel further under the ties than the other colour or colours. This will give a halo around the white area left after ties have been undone.
2. The thread or string used for tying can be dipped in a dye, taken out, hung up to dry, and then used to tie up. The dye on the thread or string will be transferred to parts of the fabric and fixed with the new colour in the dyebath.
3. By pressing folded fabric between two pieces of wood and binding around with string, then dyeing, rinsing, undoing, and retying so as to expose undyed areas to the outside, then redyeing, etc., unusual effects will result.
4. Tie-and-dye can also be done on existing self-patterned or commercially printed or woven stripe or spot patterns. Check, of course, that the existing dye will stand up to your own dyeing.
5. Dyeing tied fabrics with vegetable or natural dyes can be most rewarding. The following natural dyes are available from suppliers and include most of the well known dyes imported from abroad. They are suitable for use on cotton, linen, wool, and silk, with the appropriate mordants.

   Alkanet – red-brown, blue, deep violet; annatto – red; cutch (catechu) – brown; fustic – yellow; indigo – blue; logwood – red-brown; madder – red; weld – yellow.

   The following will be found in the countryside, garden, or kitchen.

   Bark from trees – cream to tan; bilberry – pink to purple; blackberry – purple grey; elderberry – violet; golden rod –

lemon to gold; heather – dull yellow; horsetail – green; nettle – green; lichen (*Parmelia saxatalis*) – brown; privet leaves – dull to bright yellow; walnuts – brown; weld – yellow.

All should be used with their appropriate mordants. Recipes and other details will be found in *The Beginner's Guide to Spinning* in this series.

6

Wax and starch batik

Batik is an ancient and versatile technique known before the seventh century A.D. in China and India. It reached a very high level in Indonesia, where wax batik was often combined with block printing and the use of gold and silver (*Plate 3*). In West Africa, batik was developed with starch-paste resists, stencils, and indigo.

Batik is a resist technique in which wax or starch applied to the background or design prevents a dye or pigment colour from taking on, and so colouring, parts of the fabric. Layer after layer of resist is applied alternately with dyeings of many colours to produce very rich and striking effects.

Wax batik

Wax for batik must always be heated in a double container, e.g., a double saucepan (*Figure 6.1 a, b*) or glue kettle (c) with water in the lower container and wax in the top one to avoid the risk of the wax catching fire. Do not allow the bottom container to boil dry, the wax to boil, or water to be dropped in the hot wax. It is possible to buy an electric waterless glue kettle with a thermostatic control such as the Barlow-Whitney (d).

Always allow sufficient time for the wax to melt fully. Wax that is only warm will not penetrate the fabric but will lie on the surface when cold and so flake off, allowing the dye to penetrate the resisted areas.

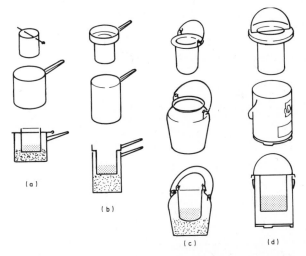

Figure 6.1. Heating batik wax. (a) An improvised wax heater. The tin containing the wax is pierced to take a metal skewer at the top and suspended in a saucepan of water, not touching the bottom. (b) A double saucepan with wax in the top and water in the bottom. (c) Woodworker's glue kettle, heated either by an internal electric element or on a gasring or hotplate. (d) Barlow-Whitney waterless thermostatically controlled glue kettle

Apply the wax quickly and, when using a brush, do not try to work it in as if it were paint, since wax cools rapidly.

Waxes and wax tools
There are several types of wax available for batik, including paraffin or mineral wax, which cracks very easily and may let too much dye on to the fabric; rosin, a very sticky wax, harder to remove and almost impossible to crack; beeswax, similar to rosin but more pliable; commercial batik wax, sold in blocks; household candles; and Dorland's Textile Wax, a cold wax used with hot dyes.

Many craftsmen develop their own type of wax. A mixture of one part of bleached beeswax to three parts of paraffin wax will give a crackle without too much flaking. One disc of bleached beeswax to six white household candles will give a satisfactory mixture. When candles are used, remove the wicks from the melted wax to avoid discolouration.

Hot wax can be applied with a brush (in various sizes, the most commonly used tool) or a tjanting (*Figure 6.2*). This is a small metal cup and spout fixed to a wooden handle. The cup

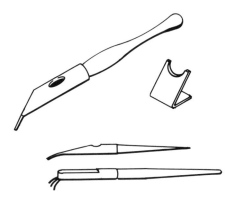

Figure 6.2. Single and multi-spouted tjantings and stand

holds hot wax. The tool is used for fine, detailed work not possible with a brush. Different sizes of spout are available, as well as multi-spouted versions.

Printing sticks or stamps can be made from strips of cloth wrapped around sticks, or from pieces of hollow tube, or from washers, etc., stuck on one end of a stick, or from the ends of rolls of corrugated paper, or bookbinders' metal stamps (*Figure 6.3*).

Figure 6.3. Improvised wax printing stamps

A large wedge-shaped brush allows fine lines or large areas to be waxed with the same brush (*Figure 6.4*). To make one, first fill the brush with hot wax. If it splays outwards, press it gently against the hot inside of the wax container so as to release moisture and air trapped inside the bristles. Allow the waxed brush to cool and then cut the bristles diagonally with scissors or a sharp knife.

Figure 6.4. A wedge-shaped brush for applying wax

Never leave brushes or tjantings standing in hot wax: it will damage the bristles or spouts. Prop up brushes and tjantings between use to prevent the hot wax from sticking to the working surface (*Figure 6.2*).

Applying the wax
The table should be covered with several layers of flat, clean newspaper with any creases or folds ironed out. Upon this lay a piece of flat greaseproof paper, and place the ironed and prepared fabric on top.

Alternatively, use a batik frame, which can be bought from specialist craft shops and suppliers. These are adjustable as shown in *Figure 6.5*. An old picture frame, if soundly constructed, or a silk-screening frame can also be used. The prepared fabric is stretched tightly across the frame and pinned to its edges. Use of a frame has the advantage that the hot wax penetrates the cloth but does not stick to the greaseproof paper on the table.

The wax must be hot enough to fully penetrate the fabric. This may involve extra waxing of the back of the design when a brush is used (not necessary when a tjanting is used for finer work).

If the wax, when applied, appears transparent and sinks into the fabric, it is hot enough to protect the fabric from the dye. If it turns opaque and lies on the surface, it is too cool, and it will easily flake off the fabric and so allow the dye to penetrate into the areas you wish to protect.

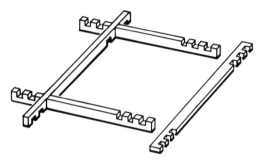

Figure 6.5. An adjustable frame for batik

If required, the cold wax can be cracked to enable the dye to penetrate to the fabric and so give the delicate veining so typical of batik. Do this by firmly squeezing, not twisting, the fabric in a large bowl of cold water. Hold the opened out fabric up to light to see the crackle. Do not dry before dyeing. Do not pour water containing wax down a sink or drain: strain out the flakes of wax, wrap them in newspaper, and throw them away.

Accidental spots of wax or wrong waxing can be removed from the fabric by carefully scraping and then ironing out between pieces of white blotting paper, or paper towels or handkerchiefs, and then using a non-inflammable proprietary grease remover.

Wax should not be applied to damp fabric.

After dyeing the fabric, the wax is removed by boiling in plain water and then in water with detergent added. Rinse thoroughly and iron. Never pour hot or cold liquids containing wax down the sink or they will solidify and can block the drain. Hot liquids should be left until cold and the solidified wax removed. The wax from plain water can be used again, the wax from detergent water should be thrown away.

Wax can also be removed, to a certain extent, by ironing the fabric between sheets of clean paper, with the iron set to the correct temperature for the fabric. It is difficult to apply more dye if the wax is removed by this method, which is not recommended unless boiling out is impossible (e.g., when using pigment dyes that require fixing by a heat treatment).

Suitable fabrics
The best fabrics to use for batik with Dylon Cold Water Dyes and Procion M dyes are those made from natural fibres (cotton, linen, silk, jute), as well as canvas and the manmade acetate rayon. Fine wool tends to retain the wax.

Fabric should be prepared as described in Chapter 4.

Marking out the design
Pencil lines used to indicate the design cannot always be removed, as they are trapped indelibly by the wax or dye. If a pencil is used, it should be a soft one, used very faintly and in dots rather than lines.

Figure 6.6. Marking-out with threads

Another method of marking is to press guidelines into the folded fabric with a warm iron before it is opened out and stretched over a frame. Alternatively, lines of cotton thread can be stretched across the fabric and fastened to the edges of the frame (*Figure 6.6*).

If the fabric is thin enough, the design can be drawn on greaseproof paper with a waterproof marker to make a strong black outline, and put underneath the fabric so as to show through.

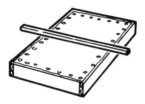

Figure 6.7. Using a wooden strip as a guide rail to obtain straight lines

Some designs can be drawn on the fabric with a sharpened candle, a white wax pencil, or a crayon.

For straight lines of wax, a strip or batten of wood can be laid across the fabric to act as a guide rail for a brush or tjanting (*Figure 6.7*).

Dyes

The easiest dyes for beginners to use are Dylon Cold Water Dyes, Dylon Ultra-Batik Dyes, and certain of the reactive dyestuffs (recipes in Chapter 12). The dyes, when mixed, can be used in a dyebath or applied to the waxed fabric in a concentrated form with a brush or a foam or felt roller.

Certain natural dyestuffs such as indigo can be used but the dyeing process is somewhat complicated.

It is also possible to use pigment colours, such as Polyprint and others listed in Chapter 12. The colours are brushed on to the waxed fabric and allowed to dry, and then the dye is fixed and the wax removed at the same time by ironing between sheets of clean paper.

Splashed and dripped batiks

To make splashed and dripped batiks (*Figure 6.8*), cover the working area with a piece of plastic sheeting; tape or pin the fabric on a frame. Drop hot wax from a brush or a lighted candle. The candle is held upright and close to the fabric, and then tilted to allow drips of hot wax to fall on the fabric. Turn the candle as it drips to obtain even melting of the wax.

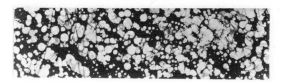

Figure 6.8. A splashed and dripped batik

If the frame is held nearly vertically, long splashes will result; varying the angle will produce different shapes.

After dyeing, the fabric can be rewaxed when dry and redyed as often as required. As a safety measure, keep a bowl of cold water on the table.

Crackled batiks

For crackled batiks (*Figures 6.9, 6.10*), either fold the fabric in 25 mm (1 in) pleats, open it out flat, and place it on the working area; or draw very faint pencil lines for the stripes. With a 25 mm (1 in) paintbrush, brush on hot wax so as to completely coat alternative pleats on both sides of the fabric (*Figure 6.9a*). Immerse the fabric in cold water in a bowl and

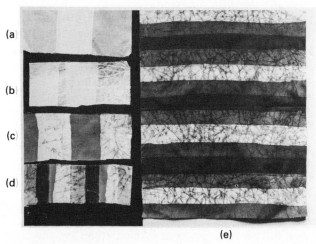

(a)
(b)
(c)
(d)
(e)

Figure 6.9. Waxing and cracking in stripes

squeeze it thoroughly to produce a crackled effect in the wax stripes (b).

Select two dyes the colours of which will give a third colour (e.g., crimson and blue to give purple, orange and dark green to give brown). Dye the fabric in the first colour.

Remove the wax by boiling off and then iron the fabric until it is dry (c).

Brush on further stripes of hot wax. These can either cross over the first stripes to give a check pattern, or follow the same direction of the first stripes but moved along so that half of the new waxing overlaps the plain stripe.

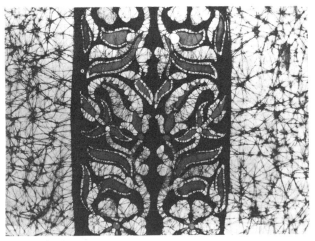

Figure 6.10. Part of a modern Indian dress fabric, showing hairline crackle

Immerse the fabric in a bowl of cold water, squeeze, etc., as before, and dye in the second colour. Remove the wax and iron the fabric dry (d).

Further stripes, dots, or circles can be added as required and dyed in another colour or colours to give many different colour combinations.

From this principle can be developed stripes and checks of various widths, circles (for which the cloth is folded into squares and opened out, and a spoonful of hot wax is poured into each square, allowed to cool, and cracked as before), and all-over patterns. It can be used to make large representational or abstract hangings, single units for cushion covers, placemats, handkerchiefs, ties, scarves, etc.

General background crackle over the whole of the fabric will give a regular texture on which a definite pattern can be developed.

Tjanting batiks
The tjanting is an excellent tool for producing lines and spots (*Figure 6.11*). It is warmed in the hot wax (do not stand it in the wax), half filled, tipped slightly backwards to stop any wax dripping from the spout(s), then taken to the fabric, a piece of screwed up rag or newspaper being held in the other hand and under the spout(s) to prevent unwanted drips on the fabric.

Figure 6.11. A length of batik fabric with a tjanting-drawn pattern. (Patricia Robinson)

Place the spout(s) on the fabric and draw lines, outlines, spots, circles, etc., according to the design. Tip the tjanting back and forwards to control the wax flow. Work as quickly as possible. As the wax empties or cools, refill the tjanting with hot wax.

Use a brush to fill in outlines with solid wax. The tjanting or a brush can be used to apply lines or 'walls' of wax to enclose different colours of dye or with gateways to allow the dye to flow out and spread in fanlike shapes into the unwaxed fabric.

Wax block printed batiks

Apart from the printing sticks and stamps already mentioned, printing blocks can be made by gluing metal washers, nuts, dowelling, sliced corks, drawing pins, lengths of string or rope, or pieces of card or plywood on to blocks of wood, hardboard, etc. The printing surface should be level. A strip of wood can be glued to the back of the block as a handle.

The completed block is dipped into hot wax on a printing pad, held there for a moment to warm up, taken out, slightly shaken to remove any surplus wax and then printed on to the fabric as quickly as possible.

To make a simple wax printing pad, place a piece of thick felt or other absorbent material in a metal or enamel plate. Stand this on top of a saucepan containing very hot water. Saturate the printing pad with hot wax. Replace the hot water as necessary.

Dye, dry, repeat, etc., as required.

Starch resist

In West Africa, particularly by the Yoruba people of the Niger area, a technique was highly developed for the application of hot cassava-flour paste by 'brush' or through a stencil punched out of old metal sheet.

An imitation cassava paste can be made by mixing 14 g (½ oz) laundry starch, 28 g (1 oz) ground rice, and 28 g (1 oz) plain white flour to a stiff, smooth paste with a little cold water. Add ¼ litre (½ pint) hot water and stir to give a smooth paste or cream. Boil it in a double saucepan for about 15 minutes, stirring regularly.

This mixture is best applied hot to the fabric and left to dry hard before dyeing is commenced.

Various other pastes, such as cold-water wallpaper pastes, riceflour, Polycell, kaolin, 'starch, and British gum, can be used. Two points are essential: the resist must be reasonably hard-setting to withstand cold dyeing but must also be able to be washed out of the fabric in hot water after dyeing.

Figure 6.12. Starch-paste crackle. Top left, strips of thick, medium, and thin starch paste brushed on to fabric. Bottom left, fabric pulled to crack paste when dry. Bottom centre, dye painted on pasted side. Bottom left, reverse side, which is not painted. Top right, fabric with dye fixed and starch removed, showing effects of thick, medium, and thin starch

An easily made paste that will satisfactorily resist cold dyes and wash out after dyeing is mixed from plain flour with tapwater to the consistency of thick batter. This consistency should be varied according to the kind of crackle required: thick paste gives a coarser crackle, thinner paste gives a finer crackle (*Figure 6.12*). Mix only sufficient paste for the piece of work in hand.

The paste can be applied with a brush, a potter's slip-trailer, an icing bag, or a syringe with a fine nozzle, directly on to the fabric, which is either stretched over a batik frame or laid on newspaper on the working area. It can also be applied through a stencil cut from oil stencil paper (a cheap substitute can be made from cartridge paper rubbed over with oil or a candle before cutting out the design). It can also be printed with very simple blocks from a pad, or by painting or rolling the paste on to the block.

Dry the fabric thoroughly. This is most important and can take longer than appears, as the surface of the paste dries out first. The fabric will become puckered as the paste shrinks in drying.

Where a crackle is required and when the paste is completely dry, pull the fabric so that the flour paste cracks.

Dyes
The most satisfactory are the pigment colours; these will not substantially affect the paste.

The selected pigment colour should be prepared as the appropriate recipe in Chapter 12 and painted all over the pasted side of the fabric with a large paintbrush or a felt or foam roller. Check on the reverse of the fabric that the dye is penetrating the crackle in the paste. Allow the dye to dry thoroughly before fixing by the recommended method. If this requires hot ironing, place the fabric right side down on clean paper, cover the back with more clean paper, and iron at the correct fabric temperature to fix the dye.

After fixing, rinse the fabric in cold water and leave it to soak for a few minutes to soften the paste.

Place the fabric on newspaper and scrape off the paste with the back of a kitchen knife or plastic knife. Wrap any scraped-off paste in newspaper and throw it away.

Rinse the fabric thoroughly to remove the last traces of starch and iron the reverse side on top of clean paper.

Add further paste resist, dye, etc., as required.

Any mixed pigment colour left over should be kept in a screw-topped jar, suitably labelled, and placed in a cool, dark storage box or cupboard.

Water-based dyes such as Dylon Cold Water and Dylon Ultra-Batik dyes, certain reactive dyes, and indigo can also be used. Care should be taken if the pasted fabric is left in a dyebath for a long period. This may soften the paste resist and so allow the dye to penetrate behind it. An alternative to soaking is to immerse the pasted fabric in the dyebath, leave it for a few moments, remove it, and, while it is still wet, place it on a sheet of plastic and leave it overnight. Then rinse, soak, scrape, rinse, and iron it as above.

Combed starch resist patterns

This is a typical West African technique which involves painting or rolling a medium-thick starch resist on plain, patterned, or coloured cloth in striped, regular shapes, or all over. While the starch is still wet, a comb of metal, rubber, plastic, or card is used to make patterns in the starch. The comb must be pressed hard on to the fabric to clear away as much as possible of the resist in the pattern shapes in order to allow the dye to take. The fabric is allowed to dry, cracked if required, and dyed, etc., as before.

Further batik techniques

The many techniques so far decribed are suitable for producing individual pieces to be used as wall hangings, decorative panels, tablecloths, bedspreads, etc. It must be borne in mind, however, that the larger the piece to be patterned, the greater are the problems involved, particularly those of size of working surface, of dyebath and containers for boiling off, and of buckets or containers in which the boiled wax and water are allowed to cool before solidified wax can be removed.

To partially overcome some of these problems, it may be possible, when planning something like a bedspread, to make it in manageable-sized units which are afterwards sewn together.

If a skirt or dress is intended, choose the pattern of the garment first, then plan the design. Place the pieces of the garment pattern on the single thickness of the chosen fabric after it has been prepared for dyeing. Follow the grain markings on the pattern when placing them in the usual way, but allow more than the normal space between pieces. Threadmark round each piece with large running stitches on the cutting line and cut out, allowing wide margins around each piece. Where curved sections are involved (e.g. armhole, neck edge, sleeve head), do not follow the curve, but cut rough square or oblong shapes enclosing the pattern pieces (*Figure 6.13*). This will prevent the curves from being stretched or distorted during the dyeing processes.

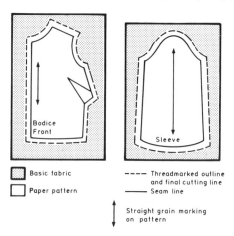

Basic fabric

Paper pattern

---- Threadmarked outline and final cutting line

—— Seam line

Straight grain marking on pattern

Figure 6.13. Placing and marking garment pieces before patterning by batik, tie-dye, tritik, or other methods of decoration

If bands of pattern are planned, possibly round the neck, sleeve edges, hem or down the front, trace the shape of the pattern piece to be decorated on to greaseproof paper, remembering to work to the seam-allowance line and not the outer cutting line. Draw the design on the underside of the greaseproof paper in a strong black outline, checking that the design will meet and match at seams. If you are working on a flat surface, place the greaseproof design under the fabric to be patterned and tape it in place, so that the design will show through. (If the fabric chosen is too dense for the design to show through, very lightly indicate the design directly on the fabric with soft pencil marks or dots.) If you are working on a waxing frame, place the greaseproof design underneath the fabric and pin or tack it in place. When patterning a sleeve or skirt section, allowances for hems must be made. Wax and dye the fabric as required.

When using several colours on a piece of batik work, it is usual to start with the palest colour and work through to the deepest. This means that the areas unwaxed throughout all dyeings will receive all the colours and will usually become a deep shade. It is, however, possible to work in a very different way, which is suitable for garments, hangings, cushions, etc., where a very dark background is important.

For this method, decide on the area to be patterned, and wax it completely on both sides of the fabric. If no crackle effect is wanted at this stage, choose a pliable wax such as beeswax, or one containing a large proportion of beeswax, and handle the fabric very carefully during the dyeing process. It should be thoroughly wetted before dyeing, as usual. If a crackle effect is wanted, choose a more brittle wax. Dye in a strong colour. Rinse, boil off the wax as before, and iron. There should now be white areas against a rich coloured background. The white areas are ready for decoration by waxing and dyeing.

For hangings, etc., this method can be used as a basis for screen or block printing, as the white areas are free to take almost any kind of patterning. Pigment dyes can also be used when screen or block printing on these areas.

To avoid immersing the garment sections, hangings, etc., in further dyebaths, design shapes can be outlined with either pliable or more brittle wax, applied with a tjanting. (The type of wax chosen depends on the effect required.) Wet the area of fabric involved, crack the wax if required, and blot off any surplus water. Strong dye solution, thickened slightly to prevent spreading, can be painted on the fabric within the outlined areas.

Lines, dots, and trailing patterns in colour can be applied with a tjanting, using thickened dye. For this technique, take a tjanting not yet used for wax, and experiment to determine the most suitable thickness for the dyepaste.

Fix the dye as appropriate. To remove the wax from small areas on garment sections, wooden tongs can be used to hold the unpatterned areas out of the water while the patterned areas are immersed in boiling water, then in boiling water containing detergent. Rinse and iron as necessary.

Bonded fabric and paper hangings

An alternative technique for larger hangings and decorative panels is the use of bonded fabrics (such as Vilene and other interlinings), reinforced papers, or other materials instead of woven fabrics. Not only is this technique useful for preparatory and experimental work, but it is simple and inexpensive and is well within the range of young children.

The method is similar to that used for batik on fabrics except that the thinned dye is painted on and the resist can be wax (applied in the usual manner with brush, tjanting, or block); an art masking fluid (such as Winsor & Newton's or Grumbacher's Miskit) applied with a pen or brush; oil crayons (particularly the softer type intended to blend easily); large kindergarten oil crayons; candles (plain wax or coloured); or Horace Hancock's wax tailoring pencils.

The wax is removed by ironing, the masking fluid by rubbing or peeling. Coloured pencils will stain the fabric as they are ironed out, and this must be considered when planning. Many designers leave all or some of the wax in the composition as part of the design. This is especially effective where the panel is hung against the light to give the translucence of a stained glass window.

The type of paper used is of great importance. It must be strong enough to stand up to the rubbing or ironing. Heavy bonds, construction papers, watercolour or fashion papers or boards, oil boards, Bristol and poster boards, and heavy papers containing various fibres (such as the decorative Japanese papers) are all suitable. The texture, such as H.P. (smooth), N.O.T. (medium), rough, as well as the colour or pattern, will affect the finished design. Metallic papers are also worthy of consideration.

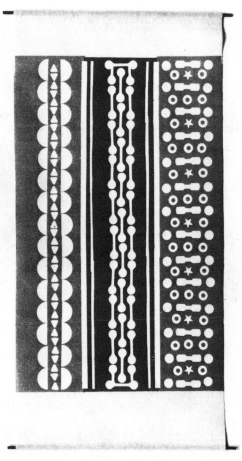

Figure 6.14. A resist-patterned hanging on a bonded fabric (Patricia Robinson)

Just as patchwork hangings can be constructed from samples and scrap trimmings, so a paper hanging can be planned to use small pieces of varied papers and surface textures, particularly from books (such as wallpaper and fabric), all glued or taped on to a board.

Each piece can be treated with a different form of resist, applied with a soft brush, pad, or sponge. Stiff brushes will scratch through the resist. Use quick, light strokes for resist or dye, avoiding a scrubbing action.

As with all hangings that are not intended to be washed, colours other than dyes or pigments can be used. Coloured inks give very bright hues but, unless sprayed to protect against fading as suggested in Chapter 3, the colours are fugitive. So too are transparent watercolours. Only blacks are really permanent in inks and watercolours.

When using bonded fabrics (such as heavyweight Vilene), the resist can be self-adhesive shapes; units cut from self-adhesive, transparent plastic (such as Fablon) in large sheets or rolls; self-adhesive, transparent tape (such as Sellotape); and similar materials. After applying the units, press them down firmly and apply the pigment colour by brush, felt roller, sponge, or screen, and leave it to dry. Add further shapes and colours as required. Dry, peel off the shapes, and fix the colour (*Figure 6.14*).

7

Printing with scraps and natural shapes

Decorating fabrics with scraps and natural materials is an ancient craft with roots far in the past. The adinkira cloths of West Africa and the tapa (bark) cloths of Fiji were printed with small stamps cut from gourds and pigments made from local gums or resins mixed with soot, natural dyes, and similar substances. More elaborate stamps were used in India, Japan, China and Peru.

The pad

The pad must always be larger than the printing unit. If a number of small units are to be used, either several small printing pads or one large one will be required. The base of the pad should protect the working surface and should therefore be waterproof, and larger than the pad. A large plastic bag (opened-out if necessary) or a piece of kitchen foil is ideal.

The pad itself should be of some absorbent material, such as felt or thin plastic foam sheet. If it is too thick it will absorb too much dye and be wasteful, and will also tend to clog the printing unit with excess dye. If neither felt nor foam is available, a pad can be made from several layers of flat newspaper.

Scrap-printing shapes

Many scraps will print from a pad. They include such things as bottletops, scent and other small or unusually shaped bottles, jars, tins, plastic containers, lids, washers, different sized sections of cardboard rolls, pieces of dowel cut to give

Figure 7.1. Examples of scrap-printing units

ovals as well as rounds, ends of matchboxes and other small boxes, corks, and pen tops. Strips of wood or plastic will print long lines. Examples of some scrap units are shown in *Figure 7.1.*

If the unit does not print easily or is not level, rub the printing surface on a piece of fine or medium sandpaper.

Natural shapes

Vegetables of many types give attractive prints. Potatoes, carrots, swedes, turnips, beet, etc., all have different surface textures when cut in half and with patterns cut on the flat surface (*Figure 7.2*). Brussels sprouts and fairly tightly packed

Figure 7.2.   Carrot printing   *Figure 7.3.*   Cabbage printing

Figure 7.4.   Headsquares with leaf-printed designs

cabbages, cut in half, give useful packground textures and individual tree-like prints (*Figure 7.3*). Cut ends of celery sticks will also print.

Other natural forms include well defined leaves such as fern, ash, hawthorn, oak, plane, horse-chestnut, poplar, and sycamore, as well as those with strongly marked veins, including chestnut, ivy, laurel, plane, and whitebeam (*Figure 7.4*). Feathers of all types, dried flowers, leaf stems, sections of cones, and walnut shells can be used.

Constructed shapes and blocks

Rolled corrugated paper secured with elastic bands or tape gives an interesting printing end (*Figure 7.5*). Pipecleaners and heavy covered wire can be bent into shapes, leaving the ends standing up as handles. Bunches of packing straw held

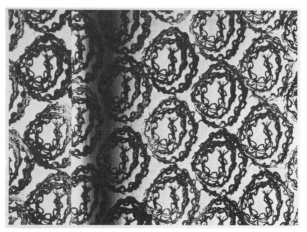

Figure 7.5. Fabric printed with a roll of corrugated paper

in one hand give unusual textural background shapes, as will canvas, thin polystyrene packing, and screwed-up paper.

Pieces of coarse canvas, rug canvas, corrugated paper, embossed wallpaper and the like can be cut into shapes and glued on to a block. Natural sponges, sections of loofah, synthetic sponges, latex and plastic foam, carpet underlay, and surface-textured or plain pieces of polystyrene packing can all be printed straight from the pad. It is also possible to print them through stencil holes cut or torn in paper, or around paper shapes placed on the fabric so that the print appears as an overall background pattern or texture rather than as a unit.

Dyes and fabrics

Pigment dyes are very suitable for this type of printing.

Any of the wide range of Lawrence's fabric inks are excellent. They should be thinned as follows with Lawrence's thinning oil for this type of work. Squeeze a 50 mm (2 in) length of the ink into a screw-topped jar; add about a dessertspoonful of Lawrence's thinning oil and stir with a stick. The consistency should be that of thin cream; adjust if necessary. Replace tops on ink and oil.

Use a mixing stick to spread the ink on the printing pad.

Unlike pigment dyes, these inks cannot be washed off brushes, etc., with water, but with paraffin.

Mixed colours will keep for future use in a screw-topped jar. If a skin forms, this can be removed, wrapped in paper, and thrown away; the rest of the ink will not be affected.

Dylon Cold Water Dyes and certain reactive dyes require thickening with Manutex to obtain the correct consistency.

All these dyes take well on natural fibres (cotton, linen, and silk) as well as viscose rayon. The fabric inks are suitable for cotton and linen, and give good results on many of the synthetic fibres; they will give a rather stiff finish to silk and fine fabrics and cannot be generally recommended for these.

The working area

A flat, firm working surface covered with a smooth blanket and a piece of plastic sheet is required.

Printing

Place the pad on one side of the working area. Spread the mixed dye over the pad, avoiding over-filling. Press the patterned surface of the printing unit on the pad. Try the first few prints on scrap paper or cloth, experimenting with ways of printing (see Chapter 13).

Place a good piece of cloth on the working area, having checked that it is clean. If using a leaf, put it, printing side uppermost, on clean newspaper. Brush dye on to the leaf, then carefully pick it up by the stem and place it, dye side down, on the fabric to be printed. Cover the leaf with clean newspaper, and gently press and smooth it with the hand, taking care not to move the leaf and cause a smudgy print. Remove the paper, carefully lift the leaf from the fabric, and place it on clean newspaper. Repeat as necessary, but throw away the messy newspaper each time.

With this method and by using a number of differently coloured pads, it is possible to build up a design in several colours all printed at the same time.

Recharge the pad as necessary. It is far better to add a little dye regularly, so keeping the dye an even shade all over the fabric, than to risk the patchy prints resulting from infrequent but heavy recharging.

When using vegetables such as potatoes or carrots, cut them so that a smooth surface is left. It is advisable to begin with a simple shape (e.g., a half round or triangle) and experiment with different arrangements and colours. A carrot can be cut lengthwise, trimmed to an oblong, and a simple pattern cut into it with a small sharp knife. This is useful for building up a pattern of stripes.

Certain vegetables (e.g., potatoes) contain starch, and reactive dyes are not recommended for use with starch. However, after a potato is cut, it can be blotted on newspaper, which will absorb surplus moisture, and then is can be used for printing. Very often, attractive textures will result; these can be used for background or can be developed as a textured print.

Experimenting with all-over patterns

It is possible to print with a single cut potato, bottletop, or other regular unit in many different arrangements.

In order to save time when designing a pattern, make about 100 good prints on plain paper. When they are dry, cut

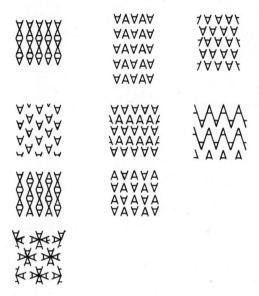

Figure 7.6. Various ways of printing with a single unit

Figure 7.7. Printing to stretched threads

them up into separate units. Arrange these on a piece of plain card in various combinations, each of 25 units. *Figure 7.6* shows some possibilities.

The linking points of the cuts on each unit will suggest further repeats. It is essential to make the final version a

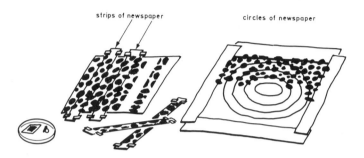

strips of newspaper   circles of newspaper

Figure 7.8. Using newspaper to give even spacing

regular repeat and not a random or straggling series of unrelated prints.

Other types of pattern include stripes, borders, explosions from a central point, draughtboard arrangements, and wavy bands.

To keep the prints in line, use threads across the fabric, taped down at each end (*Figure 7.7*). To ensure that spaces between stripes are parallel, use strips of newspaper taped down at each end. Either print between the strips or print over everything and remove the strips when the print is completely dry (*Figure 7.8*).

Figure 7.9. Multi-coloured printing pad

Figure 7.10. Scrap-printed cushion cover

Pads can be charged with two or more colours at once to give varied colours with only one printing. Replace the printing unit on the same place on the pad each time it is used to avoid merging and muddying the colours (*Figure 7.9*).

Figure 7.10 shows an example of scrap printing.

8

Printing with blocks

Blocks and pieces of printed textiles dating from c.33 A.D. have been found in the graves of fabric printers along the banks of the Nile. Blocks are supposed to have been used in India as far back as 3000 B.C., as although no textiles have survived, painted and wall reliefs show what appear to be printed patterns on clothing.

Constructed blocks

The endless possibilities of printing with scrap materials can be developed in a simple form of block printing.

For this you will need, in addition to the pad, etc., described above, some blocks of tough cardboard, block-board, plywood, insulation or pin-board, or wood; about 100 mm (4 in) square is a useful size to begin with. Square rather than oblong blocks will offer a large number of easily printed variations.

Many different printing surfaces can be made on these blocks, including the following.

Nail blocks

On the surface of a block, press in drawingpins in a pattern and print with the heads of the pins. Nails (round, square, oval, or other heads) and tacks driven into 20 mm (¾ in) blockboard can be built up into very elaborate and interesting pictures or patterns. As long as all the heads are level and closely packed, a clear good print should result. Corrugated 'dogs', screws and shoe protectors are all usable.

This form of block is still used extensively in India and the Far East.

String blocks

On another block, spread a thick layer of adhesive (such as UHU, Evo-Stik Clear, or Bostik 1) over one surface. While it is still tacky, arrange a pattern or shape of string on the surface. If necessary, tack, pin, or staple the string to hold it down (the staple or pinhead marks can be incorporated into the design). All types of medium-thick and smooth or hairy

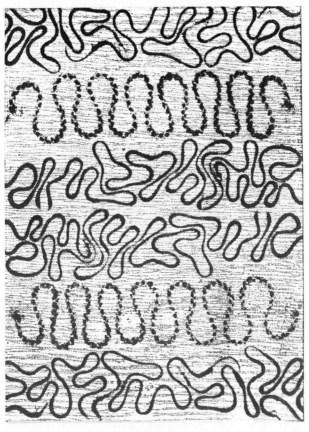

Figure 8.1. A print from a string block. The background texture is printed from a piece of corrugated paper

string, picture, blind, or sash cords, thin ropes, cloth-covered electric flex or cable, pipecleaners, woven cotton, wool, or silk cords will make pattern blocks. Keep the printing surface reasonably level (*Figure 8.1*).

Different sizes and qualities of string will vary the texture of the print. Pack the strings closely together and allow the background to print as well.

Print from a pad or use fabric printing ink with a roller and a printing plate or a tile (see below).

Built-up blocks
Other blocks can be made with washers, nuts, buttons, spent matches, etc., and small sections of metal or plastic pipes and strips all cut to the same length, and embedded in water-proof adhesive.

Figure 8.2. Making a block from dried vegetables

Dried pulses and pasta, such as haricot and butter beans, macaroni, spaghetti (any length), split peas, and pearl barley can be glued to a block. After drying, brush or spray a thin coat of polyurethane varnish over the cereals to make them last longer (*Figure 8.2*).

Glue to a block shapes cut from various thicknesses of small pieces of card, hardboard, corrugated paper, embossed wallpaper, sheet polystyrene, or felt. They can be built up, or allowed to cross over each other, or have their edges or centres textured with a leather punch (*Figure 8.3*).

Prints can be made from polystyrene blocks or pieces of sheet polystyrene mounted with appropriate adhesives on cardboard or wood blocks. The design can be cut out with a sharp craft knife or a special heated polystyrene tool, or dissolved away with certain chemicals or glue (e.g., Evostik). Embossed polystyrene tiles will also print (*Figure 8.4*).

Figure 8.3. A block made from pieces of card stuck on a wood base, and a print from it

Figure 8.4. Printing with a polystyrene tile

Pleated prints are made by folding pieces of cloth such as canvas or hessian, which are then pressed and glued on to the backing block. The ridges, wrinkles, folds, and edges will all print (*Figure 8.5*).

In all these forms of block, the surface of the printing area can be improved by gently rubbing the completed block,

Figure 8.5. A block made from coarse fabric folded and stuck to a wooden base

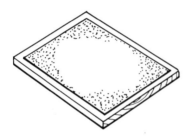

Figure 8.6. a sheet of fine or medium sandpaper mounted on a piece of board. A printing block can be rubbed face down on the sandpaper to give 'tooth' to the printing areas

face downwards, on a sheet of fine sandpaper to give a slight tooth to the raised parts of the design (*Figure 8.6*). Blow away any dust from the block, and print from a pad or with a roller, tile, and ink (see below).

Drip blocks

One of the most interesting forms of experimental block is that giving 'drip' prints. An adhesive that dries quickly without undue shrinking (such as PVA, Bateman's Household Adhesive, Weldtite, Bostik 3, or Evostik Impact) is used to drip or trail patterns directly on to the block (*Figure 8.7*). You can also experiment with old thickened paint (for example, cellulose, enamel, varnish, Japlac, and Chinese lacquer). Any paint will thicken if left for a while without a lid, and the sediment is used rather than the solvent.

Again use a block, preferably square and easy to hold in one hand. Without any preliminary planning or drawing, squeeze out the glue from the tube, or drip it from a stick,

Figure 8.7. Printing with a 'drip' block

directly on to the block. Build up a pattern and leave it to set hard. The background of the block will print as well as the drips and runs. To prevent the edges of the block from printing, place runs or rows of dots near them.

Patterns can be built up with further drips upon, across, or between the original drips. The height of the built-up portions governs the areas of background appearing in the finished print.

This is a method that is not so liable to chance as at first appears. Not only the typical 'blob and run' shapes but quite definite planned patterns are possible. Larger blocks can be used to print handkerchiefs, or four can be used together for a headsquare.

Small objects, (buttons, washers, etc.) can be imbedded in the glue while it is still wet.

Blocks can be reverse-printed in a different colour upon the first print. They can also be deliberately misprinted to one side or diagonally on top of the first prints.

Clay and plaster blocks

Clay blocks require access to a potter's kiln. Take a ball of potters' clay, place it on a plastic sheet on the working area and roll it out with a damp rollingpin. Do this between two pieces of wood about 1 cm (½ in) thick to make the whole piece of clay about this thickness, and give it a smooth surface. With a sharp craft knife or pastry cutter, mark out a convenient block shape on the surface. Take care to disturb the flat surface of the clay as little as possible. Next, press objects (such as matchsticks, bolt heads, ends of dowel, bottletops, pebbles, nails, or screws) a short way into the surface, disturbing it as little as possible. Cut out the main shape already marked on the clay and allow the block to dry out slowly. Fire it in a kiln at earthenware temperature.

Designs can be cut into the surface of the block with a craft knife or a lino tool.

Plaster blocks can be cast from clay blocks, made as described above. The design will be in reverse.

Solid blocks of plaster (or such fillers as Polyfilla) can be made in small cardboard boxes and allowed to set. After cutting the design on the smoothest surface of the block, lightly sandpaper it and print as usual.

Wood blocks

Although a more difficult technique than scrap printing, block printing enables one to translate very complicated designs into a permanent form. From the 18th century, blocks for printing were usually made from wood, the most commonly used being box, cherry, pear, and sycamore. They were constructed in layers to prevent warping. Such blocks, although permitting the cutting of very fine detail, were costly to produce and laborious to cut. For very intricate cutting, metal blocks or wood blocks with the pattern formed from metal strip or fine pins were used.

Of the woods used for blockmaking, sycamore is the easiest for beginners to use. It can be cut with better-quality lino tools or special wood-engraving tools.

Where plain, untextured shapes are required, exterior plywood can be used. A variety of hand and jig saws are available to give quite intricate shapes which should then be mounted on a backing board with waterproof glue. Holes can be cut with drills and other woodworking tools.

In block printing, the design is reversed when printed; if this is not desired, it will need to be reversed before it is traced on the wood. The simplest method is to design on a transparent or translucent paper, such as greaseproof, or plastic sheet, with a fine waterproof marker. Then reverse the paper and trace the design through carbon paper on to the block.

Backing boards should have at least one corner a right angle and one side straight to assist in registration when printing.

To prevent the block from absorbing water, dyes, and pigments, it should be coated all over with two coats of exterior-quality polyurethane varnish. If it is required to flock the block (see below), rub the printing surface on a piece of fine sandpaper in order to give a key for the mordant used in flocking.

Softwoods with pronounced grains will also give interesting textural prints, particularly for backgrounds.

The size of a block, whether wood or lino, is governed by manageability during printing. Although a large block reduces the number of repeats, it also requires much more care in printing and registration. A mistake is more obvious and more difficult to correct when using large blocks than with smaller ones.

As in scrap printing, wood blocks can be printed from a dye pad, which should be larger than the block. They can also be printed from a tile, slab or large flat tin lid, using oil inks applied with a lino roller, as for lino block printing (see below).

Lino blocks

It is customary to use plain, smooth lino at least 3 mm (⅛ in) thick. Inlaid cork or lino cloth are not so suitable. Although it is possible to use the lino unmounted, it is much easier to handle if glued to thick cardboard, hardboard, plywood, or blockboard. It is important for repeat patterns that the corners meant to be square are really right-angled.

Designs should be transferred to the lino with carbon paper. If the tracing is not reversed, the print will be the reverse of the original design.

It is useful to mark the top of the block on the back in some way so as to avoid inadvertently printing the block the wrong way round.

Tools

The tools used for cutting lino are sharp and both of the available types need to be handled with care. Always cut away from the hand that is holding the lino. Turn the lino and not the tool. A sawing board (or bench hook) is most useful (*Figure 8.8*).

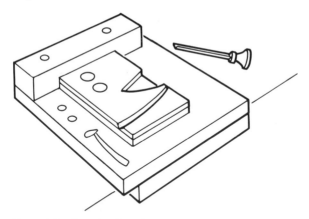

Figure 8.8. A sawing board or bench hook

The cheapest tools are those with loose cutting nibs that fit into a graver or penholder handle. Of these tools, the most useful are nibs Nos. 1, 2, 5, 7, and 8, and the graver handle. They are not really strong enough for much vigorous cutting (*Figure 8.9*).

Figure 8.9. Beginner's lino-cutting set of 'pen-nib' tools and handle

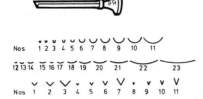

| Nos | 1 | 2 | 3 | 4 | 5 | 6 | 7 | 8 | 9 | 10 | 11 |

| 12 | 13 | 14 | 15 | 16 | 17 | 18 | 19 | 20 | 21 | 22 | 23 |

| Nos | 1 | 2 | 3 | 4 | 5 | 6 | 7 | 8 | 9 | 10 | 11 |

Figure 8.10. Lawrence's V-tools and gouges, and sizes available

More expensive craftsman's tools (V-tools and gouges) are obtainable from T. N. Lawrence & Son, who supply a very wide range of sizes, set in graver handles, as shown in *Figure 8.10.* They are very strong and can be reground and resharpened when required.

The printing pad for dyes

A printing pad, larger than the block, can be like that used for scrap printing (see above). A more professional one can be made from a piece of tough polythene stretched over a blanket pad (*Figure 8.11a*) and fastened on the back of a wood base (*b*), with a piece of felt on top to take the dye (*c*).

(a)   (b)   (c)

Figure 8.11. A printing pad. (a) Layers of blanket covered with polythene and fixed to wooden base (b). (c) Felt pad to take dye

Flocking the block

After cutting the design on the surface of the lino, the block will need to be treated in some way if it is to be used for water-based dyes and pigment colours. Lino contains a large amount of oil, which will repel the dye and give a mottled print. Some designs can exploit this effect over the whole or part of the printing area; othewise the surface must be made receptive to the dye.

This can be done in two ways. The simplest is to hold the block face down against a sheet of medium (M2) sandpaper and grind it with a circular motion and heavy pressure. The resulting mass of fine scratches will help to hold the dye.

Figure 8.12. Dusting flocking powder on to a mordanted block

The more satisfactory method is to apply a coat of flocking to the printing surface of the block. A thin coat of mordant is rolled on to the lino (which is placed on a large piece of card or paper) with a lino printing roller. A thick coat of dry flocking powder is dusted on through a sieve (*Figure 8.12*). A piece of card larger than the lino is placed on top and a book on top of that to gently press the whole for 12 to 24 hours (*Figure 8.13*).

When dry, loose flock (which can be re-used) is removed by holding the block vertically over the backing card or paper and gently tapping the back. Use a soft brush to remove any surplus flock.

Repeat the whole process, and after a further 12 to 24 hours the block is ready to use.

The chemicals used in recipes for Procion dyes will dissolve the usual mordant used when flocking lino or wood blocks. This mordant should be replaced with an adhesive such as UHU, Bostik 2, or Evo-Stik Impact (G.B.), or Sobo (U.S.A.).

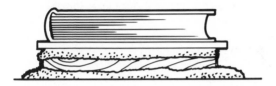

Figure 8.13. A book resting on a piece of card placed on the flocking dusted on to the printing block

If the flock surface is cleaned with care after printing, it will last for a long time. When it does start to wear off, sandpaper the printing surface lightly and re-flock as before. Alternatively, coat the block with a thick layer of bicarbonate of soda dissolved in a little water. Leave it for a few hours and wash it off.

Printing with dyes
The fabric should be fastened to the working surface with tape. Use threads or faint pencil dots to show the corners of the block as it should be placed on the fabric.

Paint dye paste evenly on the pad. Charge the flocked block with dye by lightly pressing it several times on the pad, turning it round between pressings to ensure even take-up of dye.

A newly flocked block requires 'working-in' before it is used on the final fabric. This is best done by making trial prints on newspaper or scrap cloth until they are satisfactory.

Place the charged block in the correct position on the fabric. Although fabric can be printed by hand pressure alone, better prints will be obtained by using a fabric-printing mallet, bumping the rubber end on the back of the block so as to transfer the dye from the block on to the fabric. Hold the block firmly in place with one hand while using the mallet with the other. Always bump the block the same number of times and in the same places for each print to achieve even printing. Four or five sharp bumps should be sufficient for a small block. Recharge the block and repeat until printing is completed. Dry and fix the dye, and clean up with cold water.

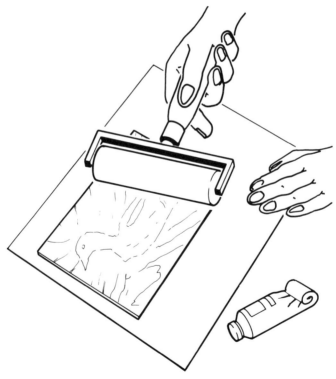

Figure 8.14. Inking a lino block with a lino roller

Printing with oil inks

When oil inks from a tube are used, it is not necessary to flock the block, unless the ink is thinned and used from a pad. Inks give a slightly stiffer print on the fabric than dyes. Squeeze out 50 mm (2 in) of ink from the tube and roll it out with a lino roller on a tile or large flat tin lid (*Figure 8.14*). When the roller is evenly inked, roll it out on to the lino without excessive pressure. When the block is covered with an even coating of ink, make trial prints on newspaper.

There are two main methods of printing. Small articles, such as placemats, serviettes, and squares, can be printed in a printing, nipping or bookbinding press (if one is available) to give almost perfect prints (*Figure 8.15*). It is possible to vary the quality of the print by increasing the thickness of newspaper under the fabric in the press. This permits the block to bite more deeply into the fabric.

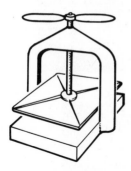

Figure 8.15. A nipping press

Repeat patterns on larger articles, such as bedspreads, curtains, tablecloths, and dress fabrics, are best printed by placing the inked block in the correct position on the fabric. The back of the block should then be bumped on the back with a fabric printing mallet held upright. Remove, re-ink, and reprint the block as required. The fabric should be marked out in some manner, as has been suggested for scrap printing.

Clean up oil inks with paraffin and rag, not water. Ink pads should be wrapped in newspaper and thrown away after use.

Further techniques

1. Uncut lino or hardened blocks can be used together with paper shapes, printing with oil inks. This method is particularly effective for patchwork, counterchange, or chequered patterns on bedspreads, curtains, etc., in several colours.

Figure 8.16. 'Progressive' prints used for multicoloured placemats (By courtesy of L. E. Hubard and C. J. Smith)

The uncut lino is linked with a roller. Greaseproof paper or plastic shapes are cut out and placed on the inked block. The block is then printed on the fabric. The shapes are removed before the block is re-inked for use with a new shape.

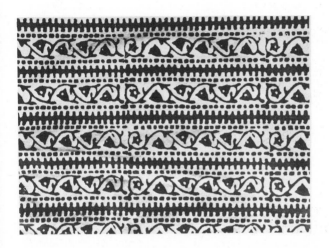

Figure 8.17. Part of a lino-block printed fabric by Yateley Industries for Disabled Persons

2. Progressive multicolour prints (*Figure 8.16*), using only one piece of lino to give quite complicated designs, are made in the following manner. Only a part of the design is cut on the lino. It is then printed in a pale colour, using oil fabric ink with a roller and tile. After making as many prints as will be finally required, the block is cleaned. More cutting is then done, the block is inked with a mid-colour and fitted over the first prints. The block is cleaned, cut again, and a deep colour is printed on top of the previous printings.

More or fewer cuttings are possible. Some prints can be made half on and half off the previous prints. You can start with deep colours and progress to paler tones. The original fabric can be of any shade since, unlike dyes, light coloured inks will take on deep coloured fabric. A different quality is obtained if the ink is not allowed to dry between printings.

The best results are obtained by printing in a press.

Plate 1 (right). A patchwork hanging using scraps, samples, and test pieces in various tie-dye techniques (Patricia Robinson)

Plate 2 (below). Tie-dyed scarves using acid dye-stuffs on silk (Patricia Robinson)

To face p.88]

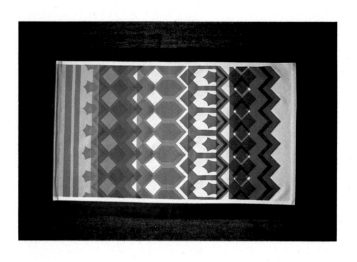

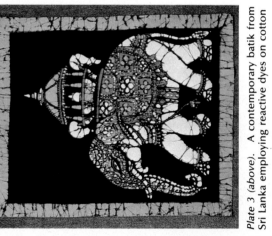

Plate 3 (above). A contemporary batik from Sri Lanka employing reactive dyes on cotton

Plate 4 (right). A greaseproof-paper screen-printed hanging using Dylon Color-Fun on cotton (Patricia Robinson)

Plate 5 (left). Screen-printed fabric using a photographic screen and Helizarin colours on cotton (Courtesy Hugh and Sophia Blackwell)

Plate 6 (right). A hanging with design units based on some of the sources given in Chapter 13 and drawn with E. J. Arnold & Son's Dye Sticks

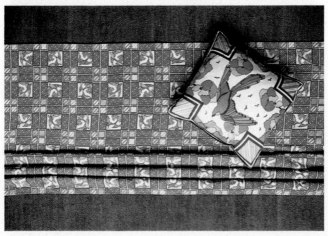

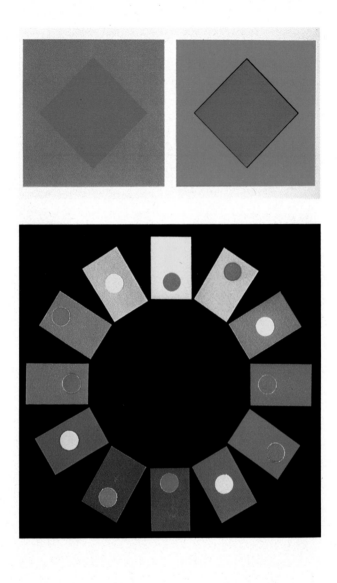

9

Screen printing

Screen printing, a simple, quick method of reproducing a design on fabric or paper, is a development of stencils. Yuzen stencils were an old Japanese form of printing, where the stencils were cut from oiled ricepaper and the free parts were held in place by human hairs. It was many centuries before the idea was developed into a screen with a 'stencil' fixed to fine-mesh silk mounted on a wooden frame. The techniques have now been so simplified that screen printing is one of the easiest methods for the fabric printer to use for single prints or all-over patterns. More than one colour can be used, and the design may be simple, using cut-out shapes, or intricate, using photographic techniques. All equipment can be bought from the suppliers listed in Appendix 1, but adequate substitutes can usually be made.

Simple frames

Smooth-surfaced picture frames that have not warped and have strong, secure corner joints can be used. Any protruding nails or projections must be removed.

Otherwise, a frame can be made from ordinary 50 mm (2 in) by 25 mm (1 in) planed, well seasoned, straight-grained softwood. Corners, which must be square, can be butt-jointed, waterproof-glued, and pinned with 50 mm (2 in) oval nails. The completed frame should lie flat and be smoothed with sandpaper before it is painted all over with exterior-quality varnish. The corners can be strengthened by metal brackets.

A convenient screen for printing small articles and all-over patterns would require four strips of softwood, each 375 mm (15 in) long by 50 mm (2 in) by 25 mm (1 in) (*Figure 9.1*).

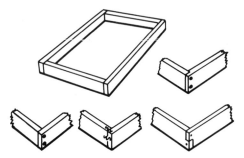

Figure 9.1. A simple screen and alternative methods of fixing the corners

Although larger screens can be made to print the whole width of the cloth at once, they usually require two people to handle. The beginner would be well advised to use a smaller screen at first and not to have screens of different sizes. This also means that only one size of squeegee will be required.

Covering a screen

The covering is commonly cotton organdie for beginners' screens, but other fabrics (such as terylene voile, screen silk, or nylon) are tougher in use, give fine detail and even printing, but are more expensive. The mesh of the covering must not be so fine as to prevent the dye from passing through. Provided that screens are cleaned immediately after screening is finished, coverings will last for a long time and further printings will not be impaired.

The fabric to cover the screen should be 50 mm (2 in) wider all round than the outside screen measurement. Fold or iron 25 mm (1 in) in all round (*Figure 9.2a*), damp the fabric, and spread it over the frame (*b*). Drawing-pin through the double edge at the centre of one side (marked *1* in *c*). Continue pinning in the order shown, pulling the fabric evenly outwards and keeping the edges level with the frame edge.

Turn the frame round and pin the opposite side in the same manner (*d*), pulling the fabric as taut as possible across the frame as well as outwards, to give a flat, drum-like surface.

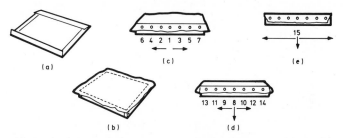

Figure 9.2. Covering a screen. (a) Edges of fabric folded in. (b) Dampened fabric spread on frame. (c) Drawing-pins pushed into frame in order shown. (d) Fabric stretched and pinned in order shown. (e) Pinning of stretched fabric completed

Continue with the other two sides, tucking in the corners neatly and pinning firmly (*e*).

It is essential that the covering is stretched as taut as possible and firmly held with drawing pins (easy to remove when re-covering is necessary), staples, waterproof glue, or a combination of these.

Masking around the printing area

On the outside of the screen, use wide brown-paper gum-strip or self-adhesive waterproof cloth tape to mask a minimum of 37 mm (1½ in) all along both sides of the covered screen, and to cover up to or over the outside edge of the wooden frame. Leave a 50 mm (2 in) margin at the top of the screen and a 75 mm (3 in) margin at the bottom of the screen (*Figure 9.3*). The margins at top and bottom are where the dye and squeegee remain between prints. The 'window' left in the middle of the screen and through which the dye will pass will be 250 mm (10 in) square on a 375 mm (15 in) by 425 mm (17 in) frame. Be certain that no dye can seep out sideways where the masking tape overlaps.

If paper gumstrip has been used, further strips should be stuck around margins on the inside. When dry, the gumstrip

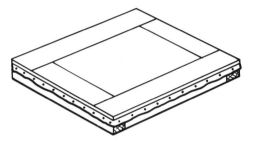

Figure 9.3. Masking the edges underneath the printing area

should be varnished all over (not the 'window', of course) to facilitate washing the screen after use. Allow varnish to dry thoroughly before using the screen. Waterproof cloth tape should not need this treatment.

The squeegee

The squeegee, used to push the dye through the screen, is best made of a hard rubber or plastic strip sandwiched between two lengths of wood which also form a handle

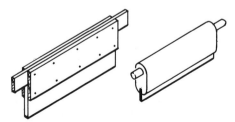

Figure 9.4. Types of squeegee

(*Figure 9.4*). It should be slightly smaller than the inside width of the frame and wider than the 'window' or the design inside it.

The small household window-cleaner shown in *Figure 9.5* is excellent for small screens and has the additional advantage of leaving one hand free to hold the screen when

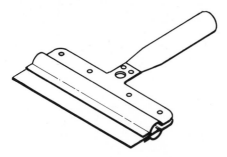

Figure 9.5. Small window-cleaning squeegee

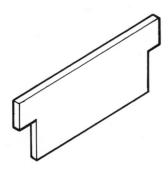

Figure 9.6. Squeegee cut from a piece of hardboard

printing. File down any sharp metal corners to avoid damaging the screen covering.

A very cheap hardboard squeegee can be cut to the shape shown in *Figure 9.6*, but be certain that all the edges are smoothed and corners rounded and that the edge of the blade is straight.

The working area

A firm, flat surface should be covered with a smooth blanket and a piece of plastic sheet on top. A clotheshorse or a clothesline, with pegs or bulldog clips, will be required to take printed fabrics while they dry.

Figure 9.7. A strip of wood used to keep one end of the screen raised from the table when more dyepaste is added, and between printings. This helps to prevent the dyepaste from running back through the design and provides a parking place for the squeegee

Extra space will be necessary to take the screen, squeegee, dyepots, etc., when printing. Other essentials are newspaper, rubber gloves, spoons, scissors, and a srip of wood on which to prop the screen between printings (*Figure 9.7*).

Dyes

Pigment dyes are the most convenient for the beginner to use for screen printing on fabric. A wide range of colours is available, they are simple to apply, easy to fix to make them washable, and they can be used on natural and synthetic fabrics. Only cold water is necessary for cleaning up. There are two main types. The first type is ready to use and is fixed either by ironing (e.g., Rowney's Screen and Fabric Printing Colour; Dylon Color-Fun; Sericol's Texiscreen) or by the application of a fixer (e.g., Arnold's Fabraprint; Reeves' Craft Dyes). The second type is mixed with a binder before use and is fixed by ironing (e.g., Polyprint; Winsor & Newton's Printex). Within each range, colours are fully intermixable.

Some ranges offer a medium or extender to produce pastel shades (e.g., Arnold, Rowney, Sericol), others an extra-thick white (Polyprint, Winsor & Newton), and one includes metallic and fluorescent shades (Polyprint).

Details of these dyes will be found in Chapter 12.

Dyes should be mixed in containers with airtight lids so that if there is any left over after printing, it can be kept in a cool place for future use. Glass jars are recommended for mixing and storage, as plastic containers (e.g. yoghurt pots) may be dissolved by some of these dyes.

Dyes are concentrated, so where they have to be added to a binder, add only a small amount at a time and stir it in well. Keep a note of the proportions in case you wish to repeat the colour.

Dyes tend to dry out to a slightly lighter shade, so try a spot of the mixed dye on a scrap of your fabric.

Pigment dyes should be free of lumps, etc., before you start to print.

The fabric

Fabric to be printed should be well washed to remove any dressing, rinsed thoroughly, and ironed flat.

It is always advisable to fix the fabric to the table so that it does not move during the printing and is not lifted from the table by the screen after completion of a print. (It is not necessary to stick paper to the table.)

For experiments and single-colour prints on small items such as placemats and cushion covers, it may only be necessary to attach the fabric to the table with small strips of tape at the edges and well clear of the pattern area. Such items can be taped to a piece of newspaper or kitchen paper before printing.

For larger work, the fabric should be fastened down to the printing surface as follows.

If the covering of the working area is one of the table coverings especially sold for fabric printing (e.g., Neoprene), the fabric should be gummed down. To do this, spread a little gum (Manutex is recommended), thinned with water to the consistency of the top of the milk, over the printing area with a soft, clean cloth, and rub it well in so that the surface appears almost dry with no visible streaks of wet gum (which would fill up the fibres and prevent full absorption of the dye). Alternatively, apply it with a squeegee to avoid streaks and blobs. Allow it to dry. Iron the fabric to the printing surface with a medium-hot iron, taking care to keep the warp and weft threads at the correct angles. Start in the centre of one end and work outwards with the iron, making sure that there are no bubbles or creases left. Check that no loose threads have crept under the fabric, as these will adversely affect the print.

Masking the screen

There are a number of ways of masking the screen to make a stencil. The following are the most usual methods, starting with the simplest.

Paper screens

Place a sheet of clean, flat newspaper on the working surface. Cut some greaseproof paper 25 mm (1 in) larger all round than the outside dimension of the screen. Fold the grease-proof paper into quarters or eighths. Cut or tear out a pattern which, when opened out, will not be larger than the 'window' area of the screen. Open out the greaseproof, and iron it flat between sheets of clean newspaper (*Figure 9.8*).

Place the greaseproof pattern on the printing newspaper and position the screen centrally on top of this. It is advisable to try out several prints on newspaper before using the screen on fabric.

Spread the dye along the bottom inside edge of the screen so as to cover a greater width than the printing area. Hold the screen with one hand and, keeping the squeegee almost upright (*Figure 9.9a*), push the dye across the screen in one firm stroke (*b*). Place the squeegee behind the dye and pull it back to the original position, leaving the pattern area clear of dye and the squeegee resting against the lower inside edge of the screen.

Starting at one side, lift the screen from the print. Prop it on a piece of wood. Leave the squeegee in position (*Figure 9.7*).

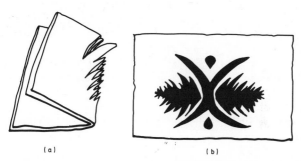

(a)   (b)

Figure 9.8. A folded greaseproof-paper mask for screen printing

The greaseproof paper should have been attached to the underside of the screen by the dye. If necessary, the edges of the greaseproof paper can be fixed to the edges of the frame with tape.

When the dye is dry, other colours and designs can be printed on top. Do not over-print when dye is still wet as it

(a)   (b)

Figure 9.9. (a) Taking the squeegee across the screen. (b) Correct angle of squeegee to screen and fabric

will be picked up by the screen and transferred to the fabric in subsequent prints.

Wash all equipment in cold water when you have finished printing, wearing rubber gloves.

Fix the dye on the fabric, following the maker's instructions, after allowing it to dry.

An alternative method is to cut or tear out shapes from greaseproof or newspaper and place these on the sheet of clean, flat newspaper, place the screen over them, and then proceed as before (*Figure 9.10*). Newspaper masks need frequent replacing, as they allow dye to penetrate after a few prints.

Figure 9.10. Torn or cut greaseproof-paper masks for screen printing

With this very simple method, it is possible to add further paper between screenings and over-print all or part of the first print in a different colour or colours. The screen can also be turned round and printed on top of the first print or to one side, and some of the paper can be removed and/or replaced. At each stage, ensure that previous prints are dry before printing on top. In this manner a simple first print may be made into a most complex one.

Figure 9.11. Gummed or self-adhesive paper shapes stuck to the underside of a screen to act as masks

It is almost impossible to remove and replace or store paper shapes without distortion. It is simpler to cut several together before printing and save the spares for future use.

Prepared paper shapes, such as gummed stars, circles, oblongs, reinforcement holes, and doileys, as well as gum-strip, self-adhesive tape, etc., can be used to form patterns on the screen (*Figure 9.11*).

Tissue and newspaper shapes break down after a few prints and allow dye to penetrate and give interesting textural patterns.

General background patterns can be obtained by placing fine thread, string, net, lace, ribbons, grasses, or leaves under the screen, as long as they are not too thick.

Candlewax screen
Melt some white household candles. Never melt wax in an ordinary saucepan – it is highly dangerous. Always use a double saucepan, with water in the bottom, which should never be allowed to boil dry. Use the hot wax to paint either the design or the background on the underside of the

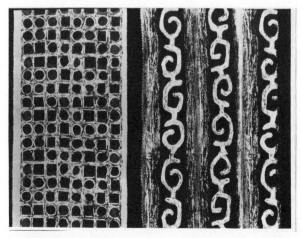

Figure 9.12. Examples of fabrics printed from candlewax-resist screens

screen. Avoid leaving ridges or lumps of wax. Allow the wax to cool and screen the dye through as before (*Figure 9.12*).

If any solid areas are porous and let dye through during the first printing, clean and dry that part of the screen and then fill in the holes with more hot wax.

To remove wax from the screen in part or completely, place the screen on several layers of newspaper, and with two or three layers inside the screen. Use an iron at a moderate heat setting and gently move it over the paper inside the screen. Change the paper frequently to allow it to absorb the wax and to prevent the iron from picking up the wax. If Terylene has been used to cover the screen, it can melt if the hot iron touches it.

Wax can also be drawn over the screen with a candle or a clear wax crayon.

A negative wax print can be obtained by waxing the design on the screen as described above (or drawing with a wax crayon). Mix PVA with water to the consistency of thin cream and paint the entire outside area of the screen, covering the wax and filling the mesh. Do not paint inside the screen. As the PVA dries, it will become insoluble in water. When it is completely dry, put the screen under hot water, which will dissolve the wax, flush away the PVA on top of the wax, and leave a stencil negative of the original design. (If the screen is held over a large bowl while this is done, the water can be left to cool, when any solids can be removed and thrown away.) Any pinholes in the PVA stencil can be filled in with a spot of hot wax. Let the screen dry before printing. A PVA-candlewax screen cannot be stripped off and re-used.

Wax-rubbed screens can be made in a similar manner to brass rubbings. The screen is placed over any raised, textured surface and then rubbed on the inside of the screen with a candle. Rub sufficiently to fill the mesh and form a stencil. The resulting prints make interesting backgrounds for further printing.

Profilm screen

The 'Profilm' method of blocking out (*Figure 9.13*) involves using a film of lacquer on a transparent backing sheet. The method of application is easy to follow and consists of placing the Profilm (lacquer-side up) on top of the design and fixing it with Sellotape at the corners. The design will show through and the parts to be printed are cut out of the lacquer only, and peeled off. Care must be taken not to cut the backing sheet. The screen is then placed on the sheet of Profilm, lacquer side to the underside of the screen, and a piece of greaseproof paper is placed inside the screen. The lacquer of the Profilm is transferred to the screen by ironing

Figure 9.13. A ribbed fabric printed in two colours from a grease-proof-paper pattern on a screen. The screen was turned round before printing the second colour

on top of the paper with a warm iron. When the lacquer is set in the screen, the backing paper is carefully pulled off, and the screen is ready for use. As the lacquer sets, it will change in colour from amber to a deeper brown. If any of the Profilm has not adhered, iron it out again. Do not use too hot an iron or it may be difficult to remove the Profilm later.

When no longer required, the Profilm is removed by using methylated spirits. Place the screen face down on a thick pad of newspaper, larger than the screen. Pour in a little methylated spirits, cover it with a single layer of newspaper, and allow it to soak for a few minutes. Remove the newspaper, turn over the screen, and peel off the Profilm. Repeat this process until the printing area is clear.

It is easier to fix Profilm to cotton organdie or silk than to nylon or Terylene, which must be degreased. This can be done by placing the screen in a sink or bath and, using a soft brush, applying a 5 per cent solution of domestic bleach. Use a circular motion and treat the whole surface on both sides of the screen. Rinse off several times and dry. Take great care: wear rubber gloves and a waterproof apron, avoid splashing on walls, floor, clothes, skin or eyes.

Simple photographic screen
The 'photographic' method involves the use of gelatine, potassium dichromate, and a screen covered as before, but with the edges not masked. Care must be taken to work in a warm, draught-free room.

Figure 9.14. Gelatining a screen

Dissolve one part of powdered cooking or photographic gelatine in four parts of cold water in a double container over a low heat.

Hold the screen nearly vertical and, using a 50mm (2in) paintbrush, paint a thin layer of gelatine across the outside of

the screen and right across the frame edges (*Figure 9.14*).
Single flowing strokes should be used, as backward-and-
forward strokes will cause bubbles which will adversely affect
the process. Do not let the leading edge of the gelatine
solidify, but avoid going over the parts already gelatined.

Prop the screen up to dry, away from direct sun or heat. A
hand-held hair dryer is very useful for drying screens, but do
not hold it too close to the screen covering.

When the gelatin is dry, apply a similar coat to the inside of
the screen. Prop it up to dry as before. Apply a second coat to
the outside of the screen, working across the opposite way to
the first coat.

Draw the design on paper, then place the screen on top,
with the gelatined outside resting on the drawing. Trace the
design on to the inside of the screen in the correct position,
leaving sufficient space between the design and the frame as
in other methods.

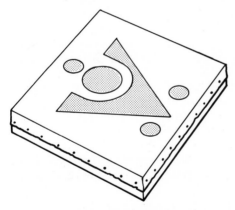

Figure 9.15. Painting a design (i.e., the area required to print) in
lacquer on the outside of a gelatined screen

Turn the screen over, and on the outside and within the
central space, paint the areas required to print, using special
screen lacquer or Japanese lacquer (*Figure 9.15*). Leave it to
dry, then check that the painted design is now opaque. Hold

it up to the light, and touch out any pinholes in the lacquer. Allow it to dry.

Dissolve one part of potassium dichromate in 10 parts of slightly warm water, and leave it to cool. Paint the outside of the dry screen and frame with this freshly-made, cold solution. Apply it very sparingly with a 50 mm (2 in) brush over all the gelatine and lacquer. Wash out the brush immediately after use.

Prop the screen up in daylight but not in full sunlight. Leave it until the unlacquered gelatine has become deep nut-brown in colour. This will take up to one hour.

The lacquer protects the gelatine from the potassium dichromate, and even after the screen has been exposed to light, this protected gelatine remains soluble in water. The gelatine directly painted with potassium dichromate becomes completely insoluble in water.

Wash the screen in hot water to remove the lacquer and the gelatine underneath it. When dry, the screen is ready to use. Should any pinholes become apparent in blocked-out parts, touch them out with a little hot wax. Provided the gelatine and potassium dichromate are painted right up to the outside of the screen, no further masking should be necessary.

This form of masking is most useful where a fine design is required, but it is exceedingly difficult to remove it from the screen when a new design is required, and it may be necessary to re-cover the screen.

A number of firms market similar materials and methods using emulsions to sensitise the screen (e.g. Dryad/Reeves, E. J. Arnold, and Sericol Group Ltd.). Addresses will be found in Appendix 1.

Marking-out and registration

Printing single items such as placemats will give experience which will be most useful in printing all-over patterns on lengths of fabric.

Never mark out with ballpoint pens, felt tips, etc., as these will not wash out or will cause patchy printing. Instead, use fine white threads stretched across the fabric and fastened to the table with tape (*Figure 9.16*). These will give points for keying the corners of the screen. Mark the corresponding points on the edges of the screen with arrows, which will be aligned with the threads on the fabric to give good registration.

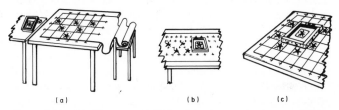

(a) (b) (c)

Figure 9.16. Marking out. (a) White threads stretched across fabric. (b) Faint pencil marks, used only if necessary. (c) Printing alternate squares to avoid transferring wet dye

If a pencil has to be used, it is best to use a very soft one and make faint dots or corner crosses (*b*).

Strips of newspaper can be laid at equal distances across or down the fabric and held with tape, printing being done between the strips to give equal spacing in a band or stripe pattern.

For an all-over pattern, it is advisable to print alternate shapes so that wet dye does not come off on the underneath of the screen and then re-mark the fabric. When these are dry, print the remainder (*c*). Alternatively, the first prints can be covered with newspaper as they are printed, or dried with a portable convector heater before an adjoining print is made.

Printing processes

It is always useful to have two people working together when printing a length, especially if the screen is a large one. One

105

person can hold the screen while the other uses the squeegee.

If printing is stopped for a short while, place damp newspaper over the printing area of the screen and the squeegee to stop the dye drying. If work stops for a longer period, remove excess dye from the screen, and add it to the remaining dye and cover it. Thoroughly wash the screen and squeegee in cold water and wipe them dry with a cloth. Before restarting printing on the fabric, make sure the screen is thoroughly dry, and make a few trial prints on flat newspaper in case some areas have become blocked.

If dye is allowed to dry in the screen, it may be very difficult to remove. After carefully scrubbing with a strong detergent, soaking the printing area with methylated spirit, or pricking out hardened dye with a needle, it may be necessary to recover the screen. It is much easier to clean up immediately after use to prevent the dye from drying in the screen.

Common faults

First prints from a screen are often rather poor until the screen adjusts to printing. *Figure 9.17* shows the most usual faults.

Unwanted spots of colour in or around the pattern area where the dye should not have penetrated are caused by pinholes which have developed in the masking. These should be touched out with a spot of varnish or hot wax.

Patchy prints are caused by the use of insufficient dye; or dye which is too thick; or an uneven printing surface; or a slack screen covering or a warped frame.

Spreading or running of dye outside the printed area can be caused by too thin a dyepaste. (Pigment dyes are usually of the correct consistency but if for some reason it appears to be too thin, add more binder or leave the dye container open for a few minutes and stir frequently. If it appears too thick, add a few drops of water and stir thoroughly.) Other causes are ridges of varnish, screen filler, etc., on the underneath of the screen (remove or smooth down these lumps); or the

Figure 9.17. Common faults in screen printing. Top row, left to right: a normal print; unwanted spots of colour caused by pinholes in the mask; patchy printing; Centre, dye which has spread or run; smudged print; marking off in the wrong places; Bottom, patchy printing resulting from clogged screen.

screen covering is slack; or the fabric being printed is not sufficiently absorbent.

Smudged prints are caused by either movement of the screen during printing or a slack screen covering (this involves re-covering the screen).

Marking-off of print in the wrong places may be because the screen has been placed on a previous print not yet dry. (In this case, mask prints with newspaper if new prints will overlap.) Otherwise, the dye has run under the screen after it has been placed flat instead of being propped on a piece of wood (as in *Figure 9.7*).

Clogging of the screen, giving a patchy print, means either that the screen has been left too long between prints, allowing the dye to dry and clog the screen mesh (soak the screen in cold water for a few minutes and wipe over when the dye has softened); or that the dye is too thick for the mesh size of the screen (see above).

Screen-Master process

A new process developed in Japan and marketed in Great Britain by Dryad of Leicester. The Screen-Master permits direct transfer printing from a drawing or other image on to a screen. This gives a screen suitable for use with water-based screen inks which are fixed on fabric, after drying, by ironing.

Further details are given in Appendix 4 on page 177

10

Other techniques

Roller prints

Composition, rubber, plastic foam, or fleece rollers can all be used for direct printing on fabric with either thickened dye or oil ink. Small rollers are the most adaptable. The harder-surfaced rollers (composition and rubber) are the most suitable for oil inks, softer rollers for pigment colours and thickened dyes (*Figure 10.1*).

Place a piece of thin foam plastic or felt in the bottom of a flat tray, baking dish, or decorating tray, spread thickened dye or pigment colour until the pad is evenly saturated, and roll a soft roller over the pad until it too is evenly charged.

Techniques which can be used with a roller include varying the pressure or the movement, 'skidding', and use of the edges; using the roller over stencil shapes; sticking self-adhesive shapes on to the fabric and rolling colour or dye over; placing torn or cut strips of newspaper on the fabric (fasten the ends down with tape) and using the roller in the spaces between them.

Thick string wound around a cardboard roll or a foam or lino roller will print if rolled on the printing pad and then on the fabric. If printed in pale shades, this type of pattern makes an interesting background on which to do further printing.

Figure 10.1. Part of a length printed in pigment colour using a roller

Comb prints

Roll oil ink or brush pigment colour directly on to a large piece of hardboard, lino, plastic sheet or bag (taped down), or the working area itself. Combs can be of the metal or rubber type used by house decorators, pieces of an ordinary

110

comb, or made from pieces of cardboard or thick plastic (*Figure 10.2*).

The comb should be used to make a pattern on the inked or pigmented area. Where stripes of two or more colours have been placed side by side, combing over the join is

Figure 10.2. Types of combs. From left to right: thin hard plastic; thick card, varnished or rubbed with wax polish after cutting out teeth; four metal and rubber graining combs, both of which can be bought from paint, wallpaper, hardware, or D.I.Y. stores; an ordinary comb

particularly effective. Stripes, circles and zigzag patterns in several colours, using combs, brushstrokes, fine lining with a matchstick, and similar treatments, are all possible (*Figure 10.3a*).

Place the fabric carefully on top of the combed pattern while it is still wet, cover it with newspaper, and gently move the hands over the covered area. Remove the paper and lift the fabric (*b*).

Re-ink or re-dye over the original pattern, re-comb, and reprint on fresh cloth as required.

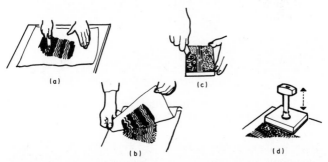

Figure 10.3. Comb printing. (a) Using a simple comb. (b) Removing fabric after printing. (c) Combing a lino or other block. (d) Bumping the block with a hammer

111

An alternative method is to roll oil ink or to brush pigment dye on to a strip or block of wood, lino, plastic, or hardboard. Use a comb to make a pattern (c). Place the block pattern-side down on the fabric, and either press it very

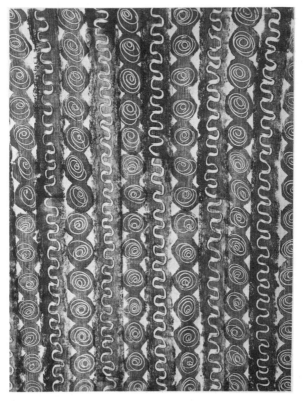

Figure 10.4. A two-colour dress fabric printed from long strips of wood using combed pigment colours

firmly by hand or bump the back of the block with the end of a hammer held upright (d). Carefully lift off the block, re-charge it with ink or dye, re-comb and re-print as required (*Figure 10.4*).

Stencil printing

There are several forms of stencilling: through a cut-out stencil; edge-stencilling or stippling; pad stencilling; spray stencilling; and splatter patterns. In the traditional cut-out stencil, the ties to hold the centres of parts of the design are part of the oiled paper used for the stencil. A cutting board underneath, a sharp craft-knife, and a piece of stencil paper or oiled cartridge paper are required. The design can be planned on a plain piece of cartridge paper of the correct size, drawn over with a black marker, and placed under the stencil paper. It can then be traced through the stencil paper. All free areas in the design must be left with ties to hold them in place.

Dye thickened with Manutex, pigment colour, or oil fabric ink can be applied with a stencil brush (of which various sizes and grades of hardness are available), a piece of bunched-up rag or thin foam, or a sponge. When stencilling a repeat pattern, care must be taken not to get ink or dye from prints just completed on to the underneath of the stencil and then transfer it back on to the fabric.

Quite large stencils can be used to print such items as handkerchiefs and placemats in one printing.

Colours can be faded in to each other or faded out and other colours and designs stencilled on top when the first colour is dry.

To clean them up, place dye or pigment stencils between pads of wet newspaper and carefully blot until most of the dye has been removed. Oil-ink stencils should be placed on a pad of dry newspaper with a single sheet of dry newspaper on top. Paraffin should be poured on this over the inked area, left for a few moments, then blotted with clean dry newspaper until most of the oil ink has been removed. Blot any excess water or paraffin off with dry newspaper and, when the stencil is completely dry, store it between sheets of dry paper. Avoid rubbing the stencil in case this breaks the ties.

Edge-stencil prints

These are made by cutting a pattern shape along one edge of a strip of card about 75 mm (3 in) wide by the required length (*Figure 10.5a*). A good shape with which to start is one based on a violin body. Rub both sides of the portion of the stencil you intend to use with a candle to make it last longer.

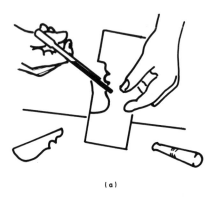

(a)

(b)

Figure 10.5. Edge stencilling. (a) Cutting the stencil. (b) Inking outwards on to the fabric

Place the waxed stencil in the correct position on the fabric and tape it down. Hold a bunched-up piece of rag or thin plastic foam in one hand, rub it on the dye pad, and smear the dyed rag lightly from the stencil outwards on to the fabric to give a fading-out appearance (b).

Alternatively, use a stencil brush to build up a graduated stipple, fading away from the stencil.

Pad-stencil prints

These are useful for small articles (e.g., placemats) or for border patterns, but they can be adapted for single-unit or repeat patterns.

Decide on two shapes (e.g., a simple leaf motif and an oval), then decide on the size of oval you wish to print. This will help to determine the width of the motif and the size of paper to be cut, and the width of the folds. If a single border is to be printed, cut two strips of greaseproof paper longer than the width of the fabric to be printed (join with tape if necessary) and deeper than the required oval. For a 125 mm (5 in) fold, cut the strips 200 mm (8 in) high, and wider than the fabric. Make 75 mm (3 in) concertina pleats across the width of both paper strips.

On one folded edge, draw half the motif shape, extending not more than 25 mm (1 in) in from the edge, and making it not higher than 88 mm (3½ in) to 100 mm (4 in) high (*Figure 10.6a*). Cut out the shape through all thicknesses (b).

On the opposite folded edge, draw half an oval 125 mm (5 in) high, and not wider (at maximum width) than 37 mm (1½ in). Check that the oval is in the correct position in relation to the motif – that is, about 12 mm (½ in) longer each end than the motif, then cut out the oval through all thicknesses (c).

Fold the second strip as the first one, but omit cutting out of the motifs, and cut out ovals from one side only, as before.

Carefully open all cut-out shapes and strips, and gently iron them between newspaper to remove creases as much as possible.

Keep all the cut-out shapes; the motifs will be required in the second stage (not the ovals, though it is useful to keep them for other possible designs).

Place the first cut-paper strip in the correct position on the fabric and tape it down.

Make a pad to print with as follows. Cut a block of pulpboard, wood, or polystyrene, larger than the patterns to be printed. Put the block into a plastic bag; fold it round neatly and tape it firmly.

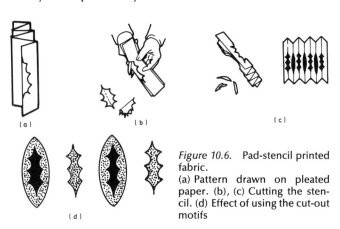

Figure 10.6. Pad-stencil printed fabric.
(a) Pattern drawn on pleated paper. (b), (c) Cutting the stencil. (d) Effect of using the cut-out motifs

Wrap three thicknesses of clean, dry cloth round the block and tape the edges to the back of the block. Trim the ends of the cloth level with the end of the block.

Prepare two colours (e.g., blue and grey). Paint the blue dye directly on to the pad, making sure that an area larger than the small motif is covered.

Press the pad firmly over one of the cut motifs. Lift the pad and check the definition of the print. If it is not satisfactory, paint more dye on the pad and print again. Continue until all the small motifs have been printed. Paint a larger area of blue dye on the pad to print the ovals.

If the pad is likely to overlap part of the printed motifs, cover them with greaseproof paper while printing the ovals, then remove the covering papers and throw them away.

There should now be a row of motifs and ovals printed in blue. Remove the stencil. While these prints are drying, prepare the pad for the second colour.

Either scrape off excess dye or blot it on newspaper. Paint grey dye on the pad, and print it several times on newspaper to make sure the grey is printing well. Place the stencil with the cut-out ovals on top of the first prints, matching cut-out ovals over printed ovals.

Put one of the cut-out motifs (reserved from the first cutting) in the centre of the first oval. Paint grey dye on the pad, and print the oval, taking great care not to disturb the motif (d).

Print as before. When the block is lifted, the motif cut-out should be sticking to the pad. Peel it off and throw it away. Repeat, using a new cut-out motif for each print.

The finished pattern will be alternate blue motifs, and blue motifs on a grey background.

A development of this technique is to cut two identical strips, with alternate motifs and ovals.

Print all cut-out shapes as before in blue. Remove the stencil and dry the prints.

Place the second stencil over the first prints, moving it so that the oval spaces are over the printed motifs and the motifs are exactly in the centres of printed ovals; tape it in position. Change the colour on the pad as before. Print the small motifs with the new colour, grey.

Use the cut-out motifs as in the previous method – i.e., place one paper motif in the centre of a blue oval and print the oval grey.

The finished result will be blue motifs on a grey background, and grey motifs on a blue background.

Experiment with different shapes and colours, and try to work out further techniques on the same principles.

Spraying

Spraying from a stencil edge will produce very interesting shaded effects. Several types of spray can be used: a small mouth spray, a hand scentspray, a decorator's pressure spray worked from a vacuum cleaner, or a more sophisticated pressure spray such as an airbrush.

The fabric is best suspended from a frame, with the surrounding wall, floor, etc., protected by newspaper or some other screening. Designs can be developed by masking or unmasking areas with paper (either lightly pasted on with flour and water or temporarily fixed with double-sided tape).

It is important that the dye used is thin enough and free enough from lumps to give an even spray but also thick enough not to unduly spread in the fabric.

This technique is particularly effective in the production of large hangings and individual pieces.

Splatter patterns

These are produced by shaking or tapping a stiff brush, such as an old toothbrush, which has been charged with dye. Another method is to scrape the dye-laden surface of the brush with a piece of card in order to splash dots of dye on the fabric.

The brush can also be charged with dye and rubbed on a piece of wire mesh or perforated metal held over the fabric, and with or without masking shapes laid on the fabrics.

Can printing

Can printing is an unorthodox technique which is used to produce lines on fabric without the usual overlaps or joins which appear between block or screen prints.

The fabric is fastened down as securely as possible with tape or by gumming. Take a small tin can and remove the top and bottom so as to leave smooth edges. Place the can on the table near the taped edge of the fabric. Have ready in a container thickened dye or pigment colour, mixed to the consistency of the cream on top of milk. Hold the can down firmly on the table with one hand and pour dye into it until it is half filled. Keep the can firmly pressed down on to the table and slide it on to the fabric. As it moves, it will leave a trail of dyestuff. Should it become necessary to stop halfway, slide the can on to a piece of greaseproof paper on the fabric, and, while still holding the can down on the paper, slide the can and paper off the fabric on to the tabletop. Place a weight, such as a block of wood, on top of the can to prevent the dye from leaking our when not in use.

A can with only one end cut off, and with holes punched or drilled in the other end (from the outside inwards) can be used to produce separate stripes.

If straight lines are required, lay a long splinter-free batten of wood on the fabric and use it to guide the can and your hand in a completely straight line.

Where the can is pulled up to the edge of the table a container should be held under the edge to catch dye and can.

Wet-on-wet printing

This is a most unusual technique, particularly in combination with printed designs. The fabric is dampened by spraying on water or a pale colour. (If reactive dyes, such as Procion M or Dylon Cold Water dyes, are to be used, sufficient chemicals appropriate to those dyes should be added to the water to maintain a correct ratio of ingredients.) Dye or dye paste or pigment colour is then applied in dots, lines or blobs to the dampened area, where it will produce the same effect as painting with watercolours or Indian ink on wet paper (*Figure 10.7*). Add more liquid dye paste to the blobs to make them spread further.

Many experiments can be carried out: e.g., broken walls of wax can be formed, the fabric dampened, and the dye applied in the part-enclosed area and then allowed to spread through the openings in the wax (*Figure 10.8*).

Another technique is to drop blobs of dye on the fabric in several colours along a fold. The fabric is then folded over, a piece of greaseproof paper is placed on top, and the dye is

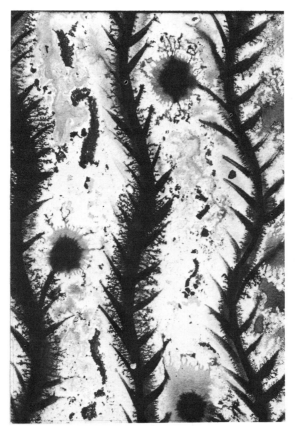

Figure 10.7. A 'wet-on-wet' fabric

Figure 10.8. A wax gateway pattern

120

spread out with gentle pressure of fingers or roller to give a characteristic butterfly pattern.

The dye can be applied from a tjanting, brush, icing bag, or syringe. It can be unthickened or thickened. It can also be applied by one of the methods described in Chapters 4 and 5 or through a screen on to wholly or partly damp or wet fabric.

Painting and drawing

Painting and drawing on fabric is easy provided the fabric is smooth enough and the dye or pigment or thinned ink is of the right consistency. It is a technique particularly useful when adding textural detail to large hangings or in combination with other techniques. Silk has always been used for this in the Far East.

The tools used will directly affect the character of the finished design. Always experiment with both tools and dyes on scrap pieces of the chosen fabric before starting final work. There are many types of brushes available, some cheap, some very expensive. It is sensible to have a few very good brushes rather than a large number of cheap ones. It is possible to buy brushes which are fine to very wide, have soft to stiff bristles, and have square, round, tapered, or angled ends, and long or short tips and handles, so it is essential to

Plate 7. (Top) Just as the eye is sensitive to different colours, so different colours seem to change according to their surroundings. Here the same shade of red appears brilliant and clear on a green ground. When placed on an orange ground, it becomes dull and drab.
(Bottom) Spots of mixed hues have been placed on the DIN colour circle (showing absolute colour sequence with additional shades). Each mixed hue appears on four very different hues. In each case, the mixed hue appears markedly different. For example, red on orange becomes dull and drab; on purple it is clear but seems to have moved backwards; on turquoise it is brilliant; on yellow it is clear-cut and appears to be in front of the yellow (Illustrations by courtesy of Der Pelikan, Gunther Wagner Verlag, Hanover; from Educational Productions' filmstrip 'Dyes and dyeing' by Stuart Robinson and Hetty Wickens)

try out several to find the type most suited to the particular technique or design to be used. A flexible brush, without a tendency to shed hairs or bristles and sufficiently resilient to return to its original shape after cleaning, will be a good investment. A tjanting is also useful for applying lines or dots of thickened dye or pigment colour.

The usual method is to stretch a backcloth over the working area and tape it down. This will absorb excess dye. On top of this is stretched and taped down the piece of prepared fabric.

The preparatory design can be indicated by very faint pencil dots on the fabric, or drawn with a black waterproof marker on the backcloth provided it will show through the top fabric.

Discharge patterns

Discharge, or bleached-out, patterns are made by dyeing a piece of fabric in a bleachable colour.

Charge the printing pad with a weak solution of household bleach (one part bleach to six parts of water); take care, concentrated bleach is dangerous. Or use a solution of Dylon Dygon Colour and Stain Remover. The bleach or Dygon should be thickened with prepared Manutex or Keltex.

Print on the dry, dyed fabric. While the work is still damp, cover it with several layers of clean kitchen paper and press it all over with a hot steam iron. The pattern should appear in off-white. Rinse thoroughly and dry; the design should then appear in the colour of the original fabric. Wash the pad and printing unit to remove all the bleach (*Figure 10.9*).

Lemon juice will also act as a discharge on fabrics dyed in permanganate of potash. This chemical will give a dull yellow ochre colour on natural fibres which is fast to washing but fades in sunlight or under a hot iron. A level teaspoonful of potassium permanganate to ½ litre (1 pint) of hot water is usually sufficient. (Too strong a mixture will weaken the fibres.) It is a useful dye for easy experimental work in discharge.

To dye the fabric, mix sufficient permanganate solution, using proportions as above, then fully immerse the prepared fabric and leave it for a few moments. Remove it and spread it out on paper or hang it above sheets of newspaper to dry.

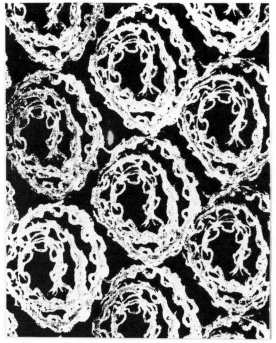

Figure 10.9. A discharge pattern. Compare this effect with the same units when printed directly from a pad as shown in *Figure 7.5*

Paint on or print the unthickened or thickened lemon juice. Allow it to dry. Rinse thoroughly in cold water.

Wherever or whatever discharge touches, it will bleach to some extent, so wear an overall and rubber gloves. Permanganate of potash is also a strong stainer.

11

Steaming

There are a number of dyes, including many of those described in the early part of this book, that do not require steaming. Among these are the cold dyes, the hot dyes used from a dyebath, and the various pigment colours.

Certain other dyes, however, do need a steaming process to complete the reaction of the chemicals and the dyes within the fibre. This is a relatively simple process and gives excellent results when using acid, direct, and other dyestuffs.

When dye paste has been block-printed or screen-printed and then dried, the dye is virtually trapped in a dried coating of thickener, lying on the outside of the fibre. During the steaming process, the damp heat of the steam is partially absorbed by the dye paste, thus creating, in effect, a very concentrated dyebath. This causes the dye and chemicals to penetrate and dye the fibre. Another function of the thickener is to help prevent the dye from spreading outside the printed areas. Over-steaming, up to a point, does not unduly affect this.

The most important consideration during steaming is to keep the fabric dry. If the printed dye is still damp when the fabric is wrapped for steaming, not only may it 'mark-off' on itself but, as further moisture is absorbed, it may be too much for the dye and thickening and so will cause 'bleeding' of the dye into the surrounding fabric. If it is kept dry, printed fabric can be left until it is convenient to steam it, and there is no need to steam each colour separately.

All steaming cloths, pads, and newspaper must be kept as dry as possible before steaming, and cloths must be opened out and dried immediately after steaming. Since they are then hot, they will dry very quickly.

The steamer

The basic requirements in a steamer are three. The first is a container to hold sufficient water to boil for about one hour without replenishing. The second is a container or upper part fitting closely on top of the water container and perforated in the bottom to allow a reasonable flow of steam to pass up, around the wrapped parcel of printed goods inside the upper container, and out through the top or around the lid. The third requirement is a source of heat, such as a gas or electric boiling ring, to go under the steamer. Care should be taken to ensure that the steamer is secure on or just above the ring so that it cannot tip over.

Many home-made containers do not give the best possible fixation because they do not supply sufficient steam.

The simplest apparatus that can be used for small articles (handkerchiefs, serviettes, placemats, head squares, etc.) is one made from a large vegetable steamer (*Figure 11.1*). An inverted saucer is placed on the floor of the steamer to spread the steam and provide a dry place on which the wrapped fabric can stand during steaming. The metal lid need not be used. This steamer is best used on a gas ring.

A larger and very satisfactory steamer an be made from an ordinary galvanised (not plastic) dustbin (*Figure 11.2*). This must be securely stood on several bricks or on an outsize gas ring placed on level ground, with some form of insulation material between the gas ring and the floor. There should be an opening window or vent to allow steam to escape outside. An alternative heat source is one or two 1½ kilowatt electric kettle elements inside the container at the bottom.

A secondhand clothes boiler can be adapted as a steamer.

There should be between 100 mm (4 in) and 150 mm (6 in) of water. If electric elements are used, they must always be covered. This amount of water should yield plenty of steam.

If possible, the outside of the dustbin should be lagged with a glassfibre jacket as is used on a domestic hot water tank.

About 75 mm (3 in) above the top of the water should be a perforated shelf or sieve. Expanded aluminium sheet is

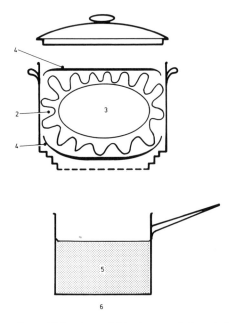

Figure 11.1. A vegetable steamer. 1, inverted saucer or piece of felt. 2, loosely crumpled steaming cloths. 3, wrapped fabric to be steamed. 4, top pieces of underfelt. 5, water. 6, heat source

excellent. It can be rested on four short stainless bolts through the sides of the container or on short legs resting on the inside bottom of the bin.

An added refinement is a second shelf about 75 mm (3 in) above the first, but this is not essential. Galvanised or stainless steel baskets in which to place wrapped fabrics are also of use.

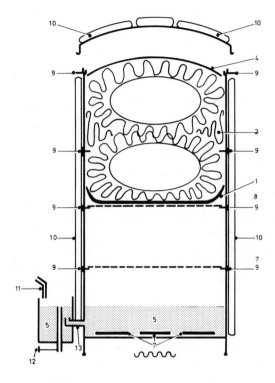

Figure 11.2. A dustbin steamer. 1, inverted saucer or lower piece of felt. 2, loosely crumpled steaming cloths. 3, wrapped fabric to be steamed. 4, top pieces of underfelt. 5, water. 6, heat source, inside or outside container. 7, loose shelf of perforated aluminium or stainless steel, resting on side supports a few inches above water level. 8, upper loose perforated shelf if fitted. 9, stainless-steel holding bolts to support shelf and lid. 10, external lagging. 11, water supply from a tap. 12, overflow pipe. 13, external cistern, to maintain constant water level

The lid, if used, should be raised to allow the free flow of steam. This can be done by standing it on two wood strips across the top of the container. It should be padded with pieces of felt.

Steaming

The package of printed fabric must be in such a position inside the steamer that it can be reached by steam but is protected from water. There will be boiling water splashing up from the reservoir of water in the lower container, the walls will run with condensation, and large drips will fall from above. In order to prevent the package from becoming saturated with water, it is most important that the fabric is carefully folded and wrapped and placed in such a position within the steaming area that no part of the wrapping touches the sides or top of the container.

Wrapping
Spread out the dry printed fabric on a clean, dry tabletop (*Figure 11.3*). Cover it with a single layer of dry, clean newspaper wider and longer than the fabric. Fold so that the fabric does not touch itself and is fully interleaved with newspaper. Fold the opposite way to form a square package – concertina longer pieces. Allow for the surrounding packing that will be required in the steamer (a dustbin steamer will accommodate a 250 mm (10 in) square). Wrap the package, or several small packages together, in a dry steaming cloth (old sheeting is excellent), making a firm but not too tight parcel: if the parcel is too tight, the steam will be unable to penetrate inside to the printed fabric.

Large steamers will take several parcels.

Packing
Check that the steamer contains sufficient water before heating. When steam is flowing freely, place pieces of underfelt, sacking, or blanket cut to size on the perforated shelf of the steamer. On this (or the inverted saucer in the other type of steamer) make a loose 'nest' of crumpled or bunched steaming cloths to prevent the parcel from directly touching the steamer walls and so absorbing moisture from the sides. Place the parcel or parcels in the middle of this 'nest', with the packing loosely bunched around, between, and on top. Place a piece or pieces of the underfelt over all. If

there is no lid to the steamer, place several pieces of thick underfelt, supported on two lengths of wood, across the top, so leaving space for the steam to escape.

It is important to pack as quickly as possible – within a few seconds. Always pack the steamer fairly loosely but right to the top. Use rubber gloves while packing. After packing, heat

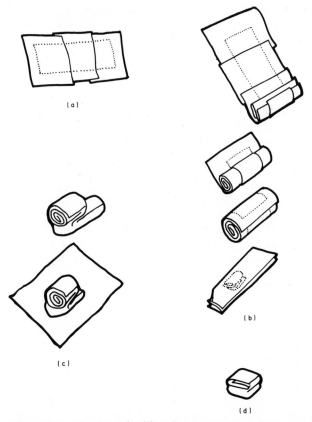

Figure 11.3. Wrapping the fabric for steaming. (a) Fabric spread on table and covered with newspaper. (b) Folding fabric interleaved with newspaper. (c) Folding the fabric the opposite way, in a concertina if necessary (d)

can be reduced for a few minutes provided that steam still flows gently.

Do not disturb the contents during the steaming process.

When using smaller steamers, such as a vegetable steamer, some craftsmen steam for one hour (or the length of time required by the particular recipe used), remove the parcel of printed fabric, open it, rewrap it in a different manner to present the inside of the fabric to the outside, top up the boiling water with more boiling water, and replace the parcel to steam for a further hour.

Unpacking the steamer
Do not cut off the heat before removing the parcel(s). Unpack quickly, shake each felt pad and packing cloth as unpacked, and place it over a clotheshorse to dry. Immediately unwrap the parcels, shake out the printed fabrics, place them directly in cold running water, and rinse very thoroughly. This is part of the fixation process and will take several minutes. It is essential to remove all the surplus dye, chemicals, and gum thickener remaining in the fabric. Do not leave the fabric soaking or the background may become stained. After this give a long and thorough rinse and when the rinsing water is clear, wash the fabric thoroughly.

Never leave wet prints in a heap. Squeeze them gently, open them out to dry, and iron on the wrong side while damp.

12

Dye recipes

In those of the following recipes which involve a dyebath, the stated proportions will give medium shades on 113 g (4 oz) of dry fabric. The table below shows the lengths of various fabrics which give this weight. Adjust the recipe as required for more or less fabric, and in tie-dyeing, base calculations on the weight of the untied dry fabric. The amount of (preferably soft) water used in a dyebath should be at least 30–40 times the weight of the fabric.

Never leave wet fabrics lying in piles before or after fixing. Always rinse them as soon as possible after fixing, open them out, and hang them until dry.

When a liquid detergent is required, suitable products are Lissapol ND, Stergene, or Teepol (G.B.), or Synthropol or Duponal (U.S.A.), used at a rate of ½ teaspoonful to 1 litre (1 quart) of water.

While carrying out most processes, wear rubber gloves and an apron.

For more detailed recipes, refer to *An Introduction to Textile Printing* (see bibliography, p. 176).

Suppliers' names and addresses are given in Appendix 1.

Approximate equivalents of 113 g (4 oz) dry fabric

Fibre	Width	Length
Fine silk	1 m (36–38 in)	6½ m (6 yd)
Fine lawn	1 m (36–38 in)	3½ m (3 yd)
Medium-weight linen	1 m (36–38 in)	1 m (1 yd)
Heavy cotton drill	1⅓ m (54 in)	½ m (½ yd)

Accolite pigment colours (U.S.A.)

Similar to Polyprint, which see.

Acid dyes

Acid dyestuffs are mainly used for wool and natural silk; some can be used for viscose rayon and nylon.

Piece and tie-dyeing on silk

1. Mix ½–1 level teaspoon of dye thoroughly to a paste with a little cold water in a large bowl.
2. Pour ½ litre (1 pint) of boiling water on to this paste, stirring until it is completely dissolved. If necessary, boil and strain.
3. Place the prepared fabric, as open as possible, in an empty dyebath. Pour on sufficient warm water to cover the fabric during the dyeing. Remove the fabric, squeezing surplus water back into the dyebath. Add the prepared dye liquor to the water in the dyebath and stir. Then add one to two level tablespoons of Glauber's salt dissolved in a little warm water, and one to two level teaspoons of acetic acid, and stir.
4. Immerse the evenly damp fabric in the bath and dye for about one hour (in piece dyeing at no more than 95°C [205°F]), keeping the width of the fabric as open as possible and gently moving it with clean, smooth stirring rods. Tie-dyes can be taken out of the dyebath at any time – from a few seconds to ten minutes – as the required colour is reached. But this may not give optimum dye fastness, which requires full dyeing.
5. After dyeing, rinse and dry as open as possible. Tie-dyed fabrics should be partially dried after rinsing and before untying. Clean up with a warm water and detergent solution.

Direct painting on silk
Reduce the amount of thickening (as given in the screen-printing recipe below) by three-quarters or until the mixed

dyestuff flows easily. Prepare the fabric as explained in Chapter 4. Fix by steaming for one hour.

Batik on silk

1. Paint on the wax or apply it with a tjanting as required.
2. Paint on the dye (or dip) prepared as for piece dyeing (see above). Blot with newspaper to remove as much as possible of the surplus dye from the surface of the wax.
3. Iron off the wax between pads of newspaper and steam as for screening (see below).
4. After fixing, rinse thoroughly in running water for five minutes (with the width of the fabric as open as possible) to remove all loose colour, and dry.
5. Do not boil silk.
6. Complete the whole process as quickly as possible and at one time.

Screen printing on silk, wool and nylon

1. One level teaspoon (for pale shades) to five level teaspoons (deep) of dye is made into a paste with 5–10 teaspoons of glycerine (reduce by half for silk) and added to ⅙ litre (⅓ pint) of hot water. Boil and strain the mixture, if necessary, until the colour is completely dissolved, and then stir it into ½ litre (1 pint) prepared Manutex, Keltex, or Nafka thickening. Leave it to cool. If Manutex F is used, reduce the hot water and use Perminal KB, etc. (see below).
2. When it is cold, add either five level teaspoons of tartaric acid dissolved in five teaspoons of water, or five level teaspoons of Perminal KB with five level teaspoons of ammonium oxalate dissolved in 15 teaspoons of hot water.
3. Print prepared fabric, then dry and steam it for one hour.
4. After fixing, rinse the fabric thoroughly in cold water, then wash carefully in a warm solution of detergent, made of ½ level teaspoon in 1 litre (1 quart) of water. Rinse in cold water. Iron on reverse while still damp.

Aquaprint pigment colours (U.S.A.)

Similar in use to Polyprint, which see.

Aqua-Set inks (U.S.A.)

These are supplied ready to print. An air-cure accelerator is available to assist in fixing the ink, with only minimum ironing treatment required. Other additives (to improve handle and body, and to give fire-retardance) are also available. The inks have very good wash-fastness when fixed, little smell, and transparent brilliant hues. They are cleaned up with cold water.

Basic dyes

Basic dyes are suitable only for piece and tye-dyeing cotton, linen, silk, wool, and viscose rayon, which have to be pre-mordanted.

Pre-mordanting

1. Decide how much dye you will require (¼–1 level teaspoon, depending on the strength of colour required) and dissolve four times that quantity (i.e., one to four level teaspoons) of tannic acid powder or liquid in a small amount of boiling water.
2. Place the prepared fabric in an empty dyebath and cover it with cold water. Remove the fabric and squeeze the water back into the dyebath. Add the dissolved tannic acid to the water in the dyebath.
3. Replace the evenly damp fabric, submerge it with weights, and raise the temperature to about 44°C (110°F). Maintain the temperature for three hours. Then leave the fabric overnight in the cooling bath.
4. Next day, prepare a further dyebath and add to it half as much of tartar emetic as was used of tannic acid, dissolved

in a little boiling water. Remove the fabric from the first dyebath, wring it out, and place it in the second dyebath for about 30 minutes.

5. Remove and wring out the fabric and instantly place it in the dyebath, which has been prepared as follows.

Cotton, linen and viscose rayon
Wear rubber gloves and an apron.

1. Make a paste with a quarter to one level teaspoon (depending on final strength of dyeing required) of dyestuff in one to four level teaspoons glacial acetic acid with enough hot water added to dissolve the dye completely.
2. Pour sufficient hot water into an empty dyebath to eventually cover the fabric. Add the dissolved dye to the dyebath.
3. Place the mordanted fabric into the dyebath, slowly raise the temperature to about 82°C (180°F), and maintain it for 30 minutes. Use sticks to keep the fabric moving and so obtain even dyeing.
4. Remove, rinse in hot and then cold water, dry, and iron the fabric.

Silk
As for cotton, but do not exceed one level teaspoon acetic acid, add one to four teaspoons of a household detergent, and limit dyeing time to 15 minutes.

Wool
As for cotton, but limit dyeing time to 15 minutes.

Brentamine Fast Black K salt

See Procion M dyes.

Direct dyes

Tie-dyeing and piece dyeing (cotton, linen, silk and viscose rayon)

1. Mix ½–1 (or more for deep tones) level teaspoon of dye thoroughly to a paste in a little cold water in a saucepan. Add ¼ litre (½ pint) of boiling water; boil until dissolved.

2. Place the prepared fabric, as open as possible, in an empty dyebath. Pour on sufficient warm water to cover the fabric during the dyeing. Remove the fabric, squeezing surplus water back into the dyebath. Add the dissolved dye to the water in the dyebath and stir well. Immerse the wet fabric in the bath and slowly heat the dyebath up to 95°C (220°F) – i.e., just below boiling point. Gently move the submerged fabric (in as open a width as possible for piece dyeing).
3. Add slowly 10 per cent (for pale shades) to 40 per cent (for deep shades) Glauber's salt (or – always for silk – common salt) calculated on the weight of the dry fabric. This should be added in four equal portions at five-minute intervals while the temperature of the dyebath is maintained at just below boiling for ¾–1 hour or until most of the colour has gone from the water – i.e., the dyebath has been 'exhausted'. Continue to work the fabric well during dyeing to obtain an even shade on the fabric.

    Never allow the dyebath to boil when dyeing silk, as boiling will de-lustre it. For wool, one level teaspoon of acetic acid can be added to the dyebath at the beginning and again near the end of the dyeing. Do not stir wool too vigorously or it may felt.
4. After dyeing, rinse, and dry as open as possible. Clean up with a warm detergent solution.

Block and screen printing (cotton, linen, silk and viscose rayon)

1. Mix one (pale) to five (deep) level teaspoons of dye to a paste with four level teaspoons of urea in a little hot water. (Urea is used to dissolve and spread the dyestuff evenly during steaming. The quantity required needs adjusting to steaming conditions. Inspect test pieces very carefully for 'spreading', 'bleeding', 'marking-off', 'fading', and any other faults before commencing on the lengths.) Add ⅙ litre (⅓ pint) of boiling water and boil until dissolved. If parts of the dye are increased up to six, then increase the urea pro rata, but have only sufficient boiling water to dissolve the dye. Strain the mixture through a fine mesh

into the prepared thickening (Manutex, Keltex, or Nafka). Stir in a little at a time until the required depth of colour is obtained. If the finished dye is too thick, add a little cold water to thin it. If it is too thin, add a little of the thicker gum. When cold, add 1½ level teaspoons of disodium hydrogen phosphate dissolved in a little warm water.

2. Print the prepared fabric, then dry and steam for one hour. Bleeding in moist steaming conditions can be reduced by using less urea, but do test pieces first and wash thoroughly.

3. After fixing, rinse the fabric thoroughly in cold water and then wash carefully in a warm solution of liquid detergent. Rinse in cold water. Iron on the reverse while still damp.

Excessive bleeding during washing off may be improved by a rinse in a Fixanol PN bath. This is prepared by adding one part Fixanol to 1000 parts of cold rinsing water. After washing off in Fixanol PN, the fabric should be dried immediately without further rinsing, then ironed on the reverse as usual.

If difficulties are experienced in obtaining an even take-up of the printing paste by the fabric, an addition of 2 per cent of Perminal KB to the printing paste is advised.

Direct painting (cotton, linen, and viscose rayon)
Reduce the amount of thickener by three-quarters or as necessary to flow from the brush.

Batik (cotton)

1. Apply wax to the prepared fabric. Paint on dye or dip the fabric. Blot it with newspaper to remove as much surplus dye lying on the wax as possible.

2. Iron off the wax between pads of newspaper and steam as for screening.

3. After fixing, rinse thoroughly for five minutes, in as open width as possible, in running water to remove all loose colour. Dry as before.

Certain colours can be fixed by ironing with a steam iron; this is especially useful in batik work or for small areas of dyeing. A temperature of 140°C (285°F) is required over the fabric for at least five minutes in any one place. Test on a small piece and wash thoroughly.

Dye sticks

These re-chargeable 'felt-marker' pens are filled with colours suitable for use on natural fibres. They are ready to use and are fixed by ironing.

Dylon Cold Water Dyes

Concentrated, intermixable, cold water dyes suitable for all natural fibres. Polyester/cotton mixtures give reduced colour results, and wool requires a special method. Thicken them with prepared Manutex to print by block or screen. 'Charcoal' will take on cotton, linen, silk, and viscose rayon in quite deep shades; on polyester/cotton mixtures, only a light shade of charcoal is obtainable.

Method

1. For each 200–250 g (6–8 oz) dry fabric weight, you will require one tin of dye, four tablespoons of salt, and one satchet of Coldfix or 1½ tablespoons of ordinary washing soda. (For wool, add 1½ cups of vinegar instead of the salt and Coldfix.) One tin of charcoal will dye 125–150 g (4–5 oz) dry fabric charcoal colour. To obtain black, use two tins.
2. Prepare the fabric. Dry and weigh it.
3. Fill a dyebath with enough cold water (hot for wool) to cover the fabric.
4. Pierce the Dylon tin with a sharp-pointed knife over newspaper. Dissolve the dye in ½ litre (1 pint) of warm water. Stir well. Add this to the dyebath.
5. Dissolve the salt and Coldfix or soda in hot water. (Use vinegar for wool in place of salt, etc.) Add this to the dyebath.

6. Put in the fabric. Stir or agitate it continually for 10 minutes, then occasionally for 50 minutes (gently for wool). Keep the fabric submerged. For charcoal, dye for three hours, stirring constantly for the first 30 minutes, then occasionally.
7. Rinse the fabric well in cold water (see Chapter 6 for batik method). Wash it in very hot water with washing powder, rinse again, and dry away from sun and direct heat. Iron it.

Dylon Color-Fun All-Fabric Paint

Intermixable, non-toxic pigment colours for pad, block, stencil, and screen printing on all natural and synthetic fabrics. They can also be used with brush and airbrush. They are cleaned up with cold water and are supplied ready to use.

Method

1. Prepare the fabric.
2. Apply the colour to the fabric as required. If the colour as supplied is too thick, it can be thinned with a little water added drop by drop. Do not overthin.
3. To fix, iron for four to five minutes every part of the reverse of the print at the correct temperature for the fabric used. As soon as possible after printing is completed, wash all equipment, etc., in cold water with a little detergent added. Do not allow the colour to dry in the screen or on the block. (If it should do so, soften it with methylated spirit and rub gently with a soft brush. Wash and dry.)

Dylon Dygon Colour and Stain Remover

A colour remover that bleaches everything but fast-dyed fabrics. It is also a stain remover for white fabrics. Suitable for cotton, linen, acetate and viscose rayon, heavy duty nylon, and wool.

Method

1. For each 250 g (8 oz) of dry fabric, you will require one tin (or one capful from a bottle) of Dygon. Remove any metal fastenings from garments, etc.
2. Fill a heat- and rustproof vessel with enough hot water to cover the fabric, and put it in to soak.
3. Pierce the Dygon tin with a sharp-pointed knife over newspaper. Dissolve the contents in ½ litre (1 pint) boiling water. Stir well. Lift the fabric out of the vessel, add Dygon solution, and replace the fabric, stirring continuously. Raise the temperature of the solution and maintain it for 10 minutes or until the colour disappears.

   For wool, handle gently throughout. Bring the solution slowly to a simmer and reduce the heat at once. Move the fabric very gently and continuously for 10 minutes. Lift it gently into a sink and cool it before a lukewarm rinse, warm wash, and a second rinse. Allow it to dry naturally.
4. Rinse the fabric, wash it in hot water and washing powder, rinse it again, and dry it naturally. Dygon should be used in a well ventilated place; avoid direct inhalation. Replace the cap of the bottle tightly.
5. For discharge printing with pad, block, or screen, dissolve the Dygon in a little hot water and add to prepared Manutex or Keltex gum. Iron with a steam iron at fabric temperature between scrap paper or cloth for several minutes. Then wash out very thoroughly. Throw away scrap paper. Soak and well wash scrap cloth immediately after use.

Dylon Liquid and Multi-Purpose Fabric Dyes

Concentrated, intermixable, hot water dyes suitable for all natural and most synthetic fibres. Wool requires a special method. Polyester/cotton mixtures and unpleated Tricel give reduced colour results.

Method

1. For each 250 g (8 oz) dry fabric weight, you will require one tin of dye and one tablespoon of salt. (Acetate rayon and

140

heavy duty nylon require two tins of dye and two tablespoons of salt. Polyesters and unpleated Tricel require three of each.)

2. Prepare the fabric. Dry and weigh it. Fill a heatproof vessel with enough hot water to cover the fabric.

3. Pierce the Dylon tin with a sharp-pointed knife. Dissolve the dye in ½ litre (1 pint) of boiling water. Stir well. Add the dye solution to the dyebath (heatproof vessel) together with the required amount of salt. Stir well. Put in the clean, wet fabric, raise to correct temperature, stir for the recommended time. Cotton, nylon, linen, silk, and viscose rayon: simmer for 20 minutes. Wool: simmer and reduce heat immediately, move continually but very gently for 10 minutes. Acetate rayon, heavy-duty nylon, polyesters, and unpleated Tricel: treat at 60°C (140°F) for 15 minutes.

4. Rinse the fabric until the water clears. Dry it away from sun and direct heat. For wool, lift it gently into a sink and cool before a lukewarm rinse.

Dylon Ultra-Batik Dyes

Highly concentrated cold-water dyes, available in three intermixable colours, suitable for use on natural fibres (cotton, linen, silk, jute, hemp, and sisal) and viscose rayon. Polyester/cotton mixtures give reduced colour results. They are not suitable for other fabrics. Thicken them with prepared Manutex or Keltex to print by block or screen.

Method

1. Prepare the fabric. Dry and weigh it. Measure out the dye (as in 2 below), and mix it to a smooth paste with water. Add 1 litre (1 quart) of warm (40–60°C [105–140°F]) water. Stir well.

2. For each 250 g (8 oz) dry fabric weight, you will require in level teaspoons: for pale shades, one dye, 32 salt, five Ultra-Batik Fix; for medium shades, three dye, 32 salt, five

Ultra-Batik Fix; for deep shades, six dye, 64 salt, 10 Ultra-Batik Fix.

3. Add the dye solution to sufficient cold water to cover the fabric. Place the wet material in the dyebath and dye for 10–15 minutes. Add the common salt to the dyebath gradually over 15 minutes. Dissolve the Ultra-Batik Fix in a little water and add it to the dyebath. Dye for 60 minutes. Agitate the fabric continuously and keep it submerged.

4. Rinse the fabric in cold water. Wash or boil in very hot water and washing powder. Rinse, dry, and iron.

5. If rewaxing is necessary after the first waxing and rinsing, then, after step 3 above, merely rinse the fabric in cold water, leave it to dry naturally, re-wax, and redye. Repeat as you wish and, when no further treatment is required, go on to step 4.

Fabraprint

A ready-to-use fabric colour that is fixed with a special fixer. The colour can be reduced to pastel shades by mixing with a special medium. It is suitable for most fabrics and is applicable by direct brush painting, stencilling, pad printing, stippling, and screen printing.

Method

1. Prepare the fabric and use Fabraprint as required. Allow the finished fabric to dry naturally and completely.

2. Brush Fabraprint Fixer liberally over the dyes or printed areas and leave the fabric overnight in a sealed polythene bag.

3. Wash the fabric to remove any excess fixer, dry, and iron. Wash all equipment, etc., in cold water with a little detergent added, as soon as possible after printing is completed. Do not allow colour to dry in the screen or on the block. If it should do so, soften it with methylated spirit and rub gently with a soft brush; wash and dry.

Fabricol

A ready-to-use transparent colour for use on natural fibres (e.g., cotton, silk, linen). The colours can be premixed to extend the range, or mixed by overprinting on the fabric. These water-based dyes can be applied by brush, stencilling, pad printing, or screen. A clear extender is available to dilute the colour strength without affecting the consistency. The colours are printed and allowed to dry; a fixer is applied and the fabric is placed in a plastic bag and left overnight to allow the colour to fix on the fabric. After this, the fabric is washed and ironed. Fabrical is particularly useful in screen printing.

Fabritint

A heat-fix pigment colour for use on most non-pile fabrics. The colour is mixed in equal quantities with a medium and can be used in direct painting, pad printing, stencilling, or screen printing. After printing and drying overnight, the colours are fixed by ironing at a temperature appropriate to the fabric used.

Helizarin Pigment Dye Colours

Intermixable, concentrated dye colours that are mixed with a binder and an activator to give a printing paste suitable for screen and pad printing on most fabrics. Rayon and nylon require the addition of a fixing agent. Fixed by heat, the prints have good fastness to dry cleaning, washing, light, and general wear.

Another type of binder combining an activator is available, as well as an extra-dense pigment white printing paste, metallic powders, and a screen cleaner.

Method

1. Prepare the fabric. Dry it.
2. Mix the printing paste in the following proportions: ¼ part (pale) to two parts (deep) dye colour to 40 parts

binder to one part activator (plus one part fixing agent for rayon and nylon).

Add the activator just before printing. Once activated, the printing paste will keep for up to 48 hours. This amount, approximately 1 litre, will screen-print about 30 sq ft of fabric.

If the paste is too thin, it can be thickened with a little prepared Manutex; if it is too thick, add a few drops of water. Do not over-thin. Allow the prints to dry thoroughly, preferably overnight.

3. To fix, iron for four to five minutes over every part of the reverse of the print at the correct temperature for the fabric used. Wash all equipment in cold water as soon as possible after printing is completed. Do not allow the colour to dry in the screen or pad. If it should do so, soften with Cleaner A50, rub gently with a soft brush. Wash and dry.

Keltex (U.S.A.)

Similar to Manutex (G.B.), which see.

Lawrence's Oil Fabric Inks

A wide range of fine-fabric printing inks, packed in tubes and used with a roller and tile or printed in a press. They are suitable for most non-pile fabrics and washable when completely dry. The range also includes an opaque white for printing on dark materials, and a reducing medium for reducing a colour without affecting its consistency.

The inks can also be thinned with Lawrence's Thinning Oil and used for printing from a pad.

No form of fixing is required other than allowing the printed fabric to dry in the open air. The inks are touch-dry in 24 hours and washable in a few days. Handle is improved if fully dried fabrics are ironed on the reverse with a warm iron.

Inks are cleaned up with paraffin, not water.

Manutex (G.B.), Keltex (U.S.A.)

Sodium alginate obtained from seaweed. The powdered Manutex Gum is made into a paste to thicken a dye so that it can be printed from a pad or block or by a screen. Manutex RS is a suitable quality for fabric printing with most dyes except basic, chrome mordant, and heavy-metal salts. Use of a thickener is essential with reactive dyes and Dylon Cold Water Dyes. A general-purpose variety is marked RS; for silk, the varieties marked SX/LD or F are appropriate.

Method

1. Dissolve one level tablespoon of Calgon in a little warm water, then make up to 1 litre (1 quart) with cold water. The amount of Calgon added will adjust the flow for screen, pad, or brush. For screen printing, one level tablespoon of Calgon will give a thick paste; for pads (blocks and vegetables), ¼ tablespoon, and for brush ⅛ tablespoon of Calgon give thinner pastes.
2. Add four level tablespoons Manutex RS to the Calgon solution, pouring it in a gentle stream and stirring constantly to break down any lumps (about five to ten minutes). Leave it to stand. When ready to use, it will be smooth and transparent. Stir it again just before use.
3. Any unused Manutex can be stored in a covered jar for a long time. Stir it well before use.

Nafka Crystal Gum

A natural gum prepared in Holland from gum karaya, which is obtained from certain trees and shrubs. It is particularly used commercially in the printing of cellulose acetate, nylon, and Terylene. For the hand craftsman, it is easy to mix and use with direct and acid dyes and in discharge work.

Normal method

Sprinkle sufficient Nafka gum into cold water, stirring continuously until a thick mixture is obtained. Leave overnight, then thin it as required. It keeps for three to six days depending on the humidity of the room.

Quick method

Boil half a saucepan of water, remove it from heat, and slowly stir in enough gum to make a thick mixture. Return to a low heat and stir continuously over a gentle heat for a few minutes until all gum has dissolved. Leave it to cool and, if necessary, strain it to remove lumps. Soak the saucepan in cold water and clean up. Thin the gum as required. It keeps as above.

Polyprint Pigment Colours

The colours are mixed with a binder, and all colours are intermixable. They are suitable for use on cotton, silk, nylon, and acetate and viscose rayon. There is a particularly wide range of colours, including fluorescents, an extra-dense white, and metallics. When properly applied and fixed by heat, the prints from Polyprint have excellent fastness to washing. Mixed dye and binder will keep for several weeks if stored in screw-topped jars in a cool, dark place.

Method

1. Prepare the fabric and dry it.
2. Mix Polyprint colour with Polyprint Binder in the following proportions: deep shades, one part colour to nine parts binder; medium shades, ½ part colour to 9½ parts binder; pale shades, ¼ part colour to 10 parts binder.

   The binder can be thickened by adding one part of Polyprint Thickener, Manutex RS, or Keltex to 100 parts of binder.

   Always use at least one part of fluorescent colours to 10 parts of binder. For metallic printing in 'silver' or 'gold', a special metallic binder is necessary. For 'silver', add one part to nine parts of binder. For 'gold', add two parts to eight parts of binder. Pigment white WP paste for dense white prints is used as supplied. Very attractive off-white shades can be made by tinting the white with Polyprint colours. Allow the prints to dry thoroughly, preferably overnight.

3. To fix, iron for four to five minutes over every part of the reverse of the print at the correct temperature for the fabric used. Wash all equipment, etc., in cold water as soon as possible after printing is completed. Do not allow the colour to dry in the screen or on the block. If it should do so, soften it with methylated spirit, rub gently with a soft brush, wash, and dry.

Printex Fabric Printing Colours

Formerly known as Tinolite Pigments, this wide range of colours is intermixable and particularly suitable for cotton and viscose rayon. On silk, nylon, and some synthetics, they are only reasonably fast to rubbing and washing.

Method

1. Prepare the fabric and dry it.
2. Mix the Printex. For deep shades, use one part of colour to 10 parts of binder; for pale shades, one part of colour to 20 parts of binder.
3. Apply by brush, pad or screen. Allow the prints to dry thoroughly, preferably overnight.
4. To fix, iron for four to five minutes every part of the reverse of the print at the correct temperature for the fabric used. Wash all equipment, etc., in cold water with a little detergent added, as soon as possible after printing is completed. Do not allow the colour to dry in the screen or on the block. If it should do so, use methylated spirit to soften it, rub it gently with a soft brush, wash, and dry.

Procion M Dyes

A brand of reactive dyestuffs which were originated by ICI in 1957. The M range is applied in a cold dyebath and gives best results on mercerised cotton and viscose rayon. On un-mercerised cottons, linens, silk, and towelling, only medium or pale shades are possible.

The dyes give bright colours in batik work on mercerised cloth.

The dyestuffs are in powder form and can be mixed in any proportions for both dyeing and printing. They should not be mixed with other Procion ranges, such as H and Supra, or with other dyestuffs. Do not attempt to store mixed Procion dyes; prepare them as required.

As with all dyes, it is essential that jars containing dyes and chemicals are kept closed and lids replaced immediately after use. Otherwise, water is absorbed from the air, which leads to a weakening of the contents and so to poor fixation on the fabric.

Acid fumes near to Procion dyestuffs will adversely affect their development.

Batik and piece dyeing – short method

1. For dry fabric weighing up to 112g (4oz), use ½ level teaspoon Procion M dye for pale shades, or 1¼ level teaspoons for medium shades, or two level teaspoons for deep shades.
2. Paste the dye with a little cold water. Add sufficient warm water to make ½ pint (keeping it below 70°C [160°F]) until a clear solution is obtained. Dissolve 1½ level teaspoons of common salt (or urea) in one pint of cold water. Mix these two together in a large shallow bowl or dyebath.
3. Immerse the prepared fabric in the dyebath for five minutes and turn it well. Add more water only if it is required to cover the fabric.
4. Dissolve three level teaspoons of washing soda (or ½ level teaspoons of anhydrous sodium carbonate) and six level teaspoons of sodium bicarbonate in about ⅛ pint of warm water and add it to the dyebath containing the fabric. Leave it for a further 15 minutes, turning as before.
5. Wearing rubber gloves, gently squeeze out the surplus dye. Then either lay the wet but unrinsed fabric on newspaper on the floor overnight (the steam from a kettle boiled for a few moments near the fabric will shorten the fixation time); or place the wet but unrinsed fabric in a plastic bag or roll it in plastic for two or three hours.

6. To remove wax in batik work, see Chapter 6.
7. In piece dyeing, rinse the fabric well. Wash thoroughly (or boil cottons) for five minutes in detergent solution. Rinse and iron the fabric. Clear up at once with cold water.

Dye mixed with salt and soda remains potent for 1–1½ hours only. Do not attempt to use it again or store it.

Avoid splashing the dye on cloths, hands, floor, etc. It stains and is very difficult to remove. Cover tables and floor with newspaper.

Batik and piece dyeing – long method

1. For dry prepared fabric (cotton, linen, or rayon) weighing up to 112 g (4 oz), paste ¼ to ½ level teaspoon Procion M dye in cold water. Add ½ litre (1 pint) warm water (not above 70°C [160°F]) until a clear solution is obtained. Add the dissolved dye to 2½ litres (5 pints) cold or lukewarm water. Immerse the prepared fabric and leave it for five minutes, turning it well.
2. Add four level tablespoons of common salt gradually over a further 10 minutes, stirring occasionally. Dissolve 3⅓ level teaspoons of washing soda (or two level teaspoons of anhydrous sodium carbonate) and four level teaspoons of sodium bicarbonate in a little warm water and add to the dyebath. Stir the cloth well, turning it over and around continuously for 40–50 minutes.
3. To remove wax in batik work, see Chapter 6.
4. For piece dyeing, rinse the fabric well in cold and then warm water. then remove excess dye by boiling in a detergent, as in the short dyeing method.

Black Procion M dye is not marketed as such but can be made from other Procion M dyes as follows. Mix 3¼ level teaspoons Navy Blue M-3RS with one level teaspoon Yellow M4-RS and ¾ level teaspoon Brilliant Red M-5BS. These can be well mixed when dry and then used as in one of the above recipes. Variations in the amount of yellow will produce interesting and unusual dark browns and greys.

Brentamine Fast Black K Salt will react with most Procion dyes to produce rich, dark brown shades. After waxing and dyeing in batik work, and before fixation, the Brentamine should be painted on to the fabric or the fabric dipped into a solution of Brentamine. It can, of course, be resisted by wax, or painted on with a brush if thickened with prepared Manutex RS or Keltex 5 per cent. Typical changes are Procion Brilliant Red M-2B to a reddish brown, Procion Yellow M-R to a yellowish brown, and Procion Blue M-3G to a chocolate brown.

Prepare the solution either by dissolving one level teaspoon of Brentamine in ⅓ litre (⅔ pint) of water; or by dissolving one or two level teaspoons of Brentamine in 2½ level teaspoons of acetic acid with 6½ level teaspoons of water and 1½ level teaspoons of Manutex. Avoid too strong a solution of Brentamine or it may obliterate the pattern. Development takes place very quickly, and the cloth is then washed or boiled.

Pad, block, and screen printing
As particular patterns will use more or less of a dye paste, it is not possible to assess the length of fabric that will require a given amount of dye paste. The following recipe will make about ½ litre (1 pint) dye paste ready for printing. Use one level teaspoon Procion M for pale shades, three level teaspoons for medium shades, or five level teaspoons for deep shades.

1. Paste the dye with a little cold water. Dissolve 10 level teaspoons of urea in ¼ litre (½ pint) of water, which can be heated, but not above 70°C (160°F). Dissolve the dye paste in the dissolved urea liquor. Slowly stir this mixture into 280 g (10 oz) of Manutex RS 5 per cent thickening. This will keep as it is for several days.
2. Just before printing, stir in the alkali. This is either 1½ level teaspoons of sodium bicarbonate pasted in a little cold water if fixation method is (a), (b) or (c), or ½ level teaspoon of anhydrous sodium carbonate and one level teaspoon of sodium bicarbonate pasted in a little cold water if fixation method is (d).

After alkali is added, the dye paste will remain at full strength for one to 1½ hours only.

3. Print on the prepared fabric and dry it. Then, to fix it, (a) steam it for five to 10 minutes, or (b) bake for five minutes at 140°C in an ordinary electric oven, or (c) iron five minutes at 140°C on the reverse with a steam iron, or (d) hang it in the air for 24–48 hours in a warm, humid atmosphere (boil a kettle in the room for some moments).

4. After fixing, rinse the fabric thoroughly in running water for five minutes in as open a width as possible to remove all the loose colour. Boil or wash for five minutes in clean water; repeat the boiling with fresh water if required. If necessary, boil or wash for five minutes in a detergent solution. Rinse and dry the fabric.

Thorough washing is essential to complete the printing process. Never leave the printed fabric soaking or half washed, but continue until the whites are clear.

An alternative method is to scour the fabric thoroughly, and soak it for one minute in a cold solution of four teaspoons of washing soda crystals to one pint of water. Squeeze out the fabric, dry and iron it ready for printing. The Procion M print paste should then be applied without the alkali in 2 above. After printing, dry and fix as in 3 above. Clear up at once with cold water.

Direct painting

The above recipes that include thickening can all be used, but the amount of thickening should be halved, or altered until the dye paste flows from the brush. They will give good results on cotton (particularly mercerised), linen, and rayon.

For silk and chlorinated wool, Manutex F thickening gives better definition to prints than Manutex RS. On silks and wools, steaming is advised rather than any other method of fixing, steaming time should be the full 10 minutes, and the steam should be as dry as possible. If steam is rather wet then decrease the amount of urea in the recipe. Omit the sodium bicarbonate when printing on wool, and do not increase the alkali at all when printing on silk.

Reactive dyes

See Procion M Dyes.

Reeves Craft Dyes

These are supplied ready to use, are intermixable and applicable by brush, batik, pad, stencilling, and screen printing on a wide variety of fabrics. An extender is available to obtain pale shades.

Method

1. Prepare the fabric.
2. Use the dyes are required. Allow the fabric to dry naturally and completely.
3. Spread the fixer over the coloured areas with a plastic ruler or similar spatula. Then roll up the fabric and place it in a polythene bag for four or more hours in order to allow the fixer to dry very slowly.
4. Remove the fabric from the bag, wash and rinse it untill no excess colour appears in the water. Dry and iron it. Clean up with cold water immediately after the fabric is printed.

Rowney Fabric Printing Dyes

See Screen and Fabric Printing Colours.

Screen and Fabric Printing Colours

Originally known as Rowney Fabric Printing Dyes, these are an acrylic-based range of intermixable pigment colours. They are suitable for cotton, silk, linen, other natural fibres, and certain synthetics (e.g., nylon, Orlon, Dacron). They are supplied ready to use. A medium is available as an extender to make the colour more transparent.

Method

1. Prepare the fabric. Dry it.
2. Apply the colour by screen, block, stencil, brush, or pad as required. If the colour as supplied is too thick, it can be thinned with a little water, added drop by drop; do not overthin. When printing with a block, a pad will be found to be better than a roller. In handprinting and stencilling on certain fabrics, care must be taken to avoid streakiness. Allow the prints to dry thoroughly, preferably overnight.
3. To fix, iron for four to five minutes every part of the reverse of the print at the correct temperature for the fabric used. Wash all equipment, etc., in cold water with a little detergent added as soon as possible after printing is completed. Do not allow the colour to dry in the screen or on the block. If it should do so, soften with methylated spirit, rub gently with a soft brush, wash, and dry.

Screen Printing Ink

A water-based colour for natural fibres, fixed on the fabric by ironing. It is supplied ready to use, and an extender is available to reduce colour strength. It is used like Screen and Fabric Printing Colours.

Texiscreen Colours

These are suitable for most fabrics and have a wide range of colours, including an opaque white and fluorescent colours. After a heat treatment, the fabrics retain their original soft 'hand' and are washfast (wool is slightly below other fibres in this respect). They are supplied ready for use and are non-toxic. An extender base is available for mixing with any colour to produce a pale shade. They are applied similarly to Screen and Fabric Printing Colours.

Thinned ink

See Lawrence's Oil Fabric Inks.

Tinolite Pigment Dyestuffs

See Printex Fabric Printing Colours.

Versatex Textile Paint (U.S.A.)

Ready mixed, ready-to-use pigment colours that are water-soluble and non-toxic in a wide variety of colours. The range includes an extender to pale but not thin or whiten the colour, and a binder to improve fastness on nylon, acrylic, and acetate fabrics.

Method

1. Prepare the fabric.
2. Apply the colour to the fabric as required, using direct brush painting, screening, stencilling, a pad, batik, or (when thinned) airbrush. Allow it to dry before fixing. This will take from 40 minutes to two hours. If the colour is too thick, it can be thinned with a little water added drop by drop. Do not overthin it.
3. To fix, iron or otherwise heat-treat every part of the reverse of the print at the correct temperature for the fabric used. The fabric should be able to withstand the 120°C (250°F) minimum temperature required to set the colours. When ironing, go over each square foot for 20 to 30 seconds. Wash all equipment, etc., in cold water as soon as possible after printing. Do not allow the colours to dry in a screen.

Versatex Air-Brush Ink (U.S.A.)

A concentrated ink specially formulated for spraying on prepared fabric or applying by a fine brush. After drying, the colours are made washfast by a heat treatment such as ironing or tumbling in a hot dryer.

13

Design sources and techniques

Many of the descriptions of methods in this book refer to a form of design which arises from the particular technique used. It is most important to exploit the qualities of the methods, tools, and fabric used rather than to impose a design not related to those qualities.

A pattern suitable for fine silk may not be suitable for a heavier linen, cotton, or wool cloth or even a heavier silk. Similarly, draped fabrics (curtains, clothes, headsquares) require a different type of pattern from flat fabrics (hangings, upholstery, placemats).

In designing, simple ideas are often the best. To provide inspiration to work from, it is useful to build up a collection of sources such as pictures, advertisements, fabric samples, photographs, labels, sales and travel literature, postcards, and samples of colour, texture, and shape.

Design sources

The following are the four main groups of sources available to designers.

Natural sources
These are, in some ways, the easiest sources to obtain, but they are not necessarily the easiest to translate into a two-dimensional pattern or unit. They include the following.

Plants, leaves, grasses, flowers, mosses, ferns, cacti, trees, twigs, branches, fruits, vegetables, rock formations, tree sections, seedheads, cobwebs, feathers, fossils, shells, seaweed, leaf and fish skeletons, birds' eggs, frost patterns, fingerprints, animals, insects, reptiles, caterpillars, tropical fish, marine plants and animals, wings, bark rubbings, wood grain, rock markings, marble, snakeskins, crystalline and precious or semi-precious stones, seashore markings, wave shapes, magnetic fields, oil-on-water patterns, sea spray and foam (*Figure 13.1*).

Helpful books include the following.

Bager B. *Naturen som formgivare* Nordisk Rotogravyr, Stockholm, 1961. (Excellent photographs of dried seedheads. English edition available.)

Barthlott W. *Cacti* Thames & Hudson, London, 1979.

Brightman F. H. *Oxford Book of Flowerless Plants* O.U.P., London, 1979.

Hamlin, Bishop, and Woolley *Mineral Rocks and Fossils* Hamlyn, London, 1980.

Hardy A. *The Open Sea* Collins, London.

Keble Martin W. *The Concise British Flora in Colour* Ebury Press and Michael Joseph, London, 1976.

Mordy *The Fossil World* Hamlyn, London, 1977.

Scheffer V. B. *Messages from the Shore* Pacific Search Press, Seattle, Washington, 1977.

Wildsmith B. *Birds* and *Fishes* and *Wild Animals* (and many other illustrated books for children by this artist) O.U.P., London.

Yonge C. *The Sea Shore* Collins, London.

Historical sources

These are often partly translated in that they can be at one or more stages removed from their sources. Among them are the following.

Figure 13.1. Natural design sources. (a) Peacock's feathers. (b) Polished pebbles. (c) Stylised flowers. (d) Spider's web. (e) Lily, Crimson Beauty. (f) Heath fritillary butterfly. (g) Poppy seedheads. (h) Fossil ammonite. (i) Sunflower

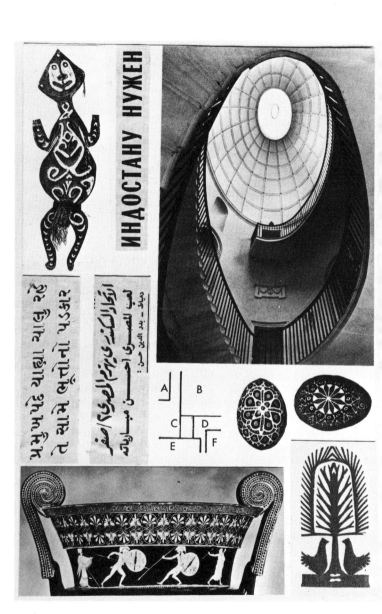

ИНДОСТАНУ НУЖЕН

158

Alphabets, (particularly Chinese, Japanese, Turkish, and other oriental examples), manuscript illustrations, Egyptian hieroglyphs and tablet markings, pottery decoration (especially Chinese, Japanese, Greek, and Central American), textile decoration (such as Indian tie-and-dye, Javanese batik, oriental rugs, and embroidery), African carvings, American Indian decoration on wigwams, blankets, hides, and totem poles, Oceanic decoration on weapons, canoes, houses, tapa cloth, and many other artefacts, African adinkira cloths, architectural shapes (especially Russian, Chinese, Byzantine, Indian, Japanese and Central American), Mexican pre-conquest 'magic' books, heraldic devices, cave paintings, Chinese, Polish and Vietnamese paper cuts, brass rubbings, Chinese tomb rubbings, engravings on Celtic, Anglo-Saxon, and other jewellery, carvings on early boxes and chests, Victorian fans, valentines, lace, playing cards, crochet, combs, weapons (particularly oriental ones), pargetting, stagecoaches and trains (wheels, brasses, shape), mosaics, boat shapes, early machines (balloons, aeroplanes, bicycles, trains, looms, spinning wheels). Figure 13.2 shows some examples.

Helpful books include the following.

Bennett W. C. *Ancient Arts of the Andes* Museum of Modern Art, N.Y.

Encisco J. *Design Motifs of Ancient Mexico* Constable, London, 1947.

Koch R. *The Book of Signs* Dover, N.Y., 1930.

Williams G. *African Designs from Traditional Sources* Dover, N.Y., 1971.

Microscopic sources
These can be a most valuable inspiration in designing. Many are available as microscopic slides, including molecular

Figure 13.2. Historical design sources. (a) Polynesian carving. (b) The dome over the staircase at Sharpham House. (c) Headlines. (d) Moravian painted and etched Easter eggs. (e) An Attic red-figured krater, c. 490 B.C. (f) Polish paper-cut

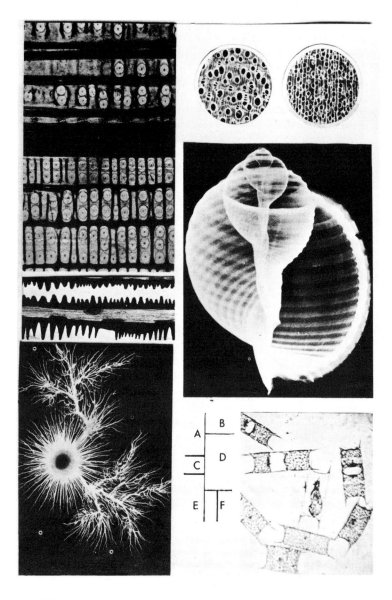

structures, diatoms, cross-sections, cells, snowflakes, textile fibres, and parts of insects (e.g., butterfly wings) (*Figure 13.3*).

Books containing microphotographs include the following.

Bentley W. A. and Humphreys W. J. *Snow Crystals* Dover, N.Y., 1962.

Bergamini D. *The Universe* Time-Life International, N.Y., 1962.

Hurry S. W. *The Microstructure of Cells* Murray, London, 1965.

Pfeiffer J. *The Cell* Time-Life International, N.Y., 1965.

Other sources

Other sources often of use include intricate manmade objects (watches, cast and wrought iron, musical boxes and instruments, sewing machines, calculators, sextants), aerial photographs, blueprints, architects' drawings, trademarks, modern abstract paintings, 'constructions', and sculpture, mathematical shapes, fireworks, blots, computer tapes and cards, piano and Jacquard rolls and cards, geometric shapes, tool shapes, road signs, Spirograph designs, springs, lines drawn on wet blotting paper or cartridge paper, contour lines, star galaxies, marbled papers, armour, kaleidoscopes, glasswear shapes (*Figure 13.4*).

Books of general use include the following titles.

Aldrid C. *Jewels of the Pharaohs* Thames & Hudson, London, 1978.

Anderson D. *Elements of Design* Holt Reinhart, London, 1961.

Beitler and Lockhart *Design for You* John Wiley, London, 1965.

Justema W. *Pattern: A Historical Panorama* Elek, London, 1976.

Figure 13.3. Microscopic design sources. (a) Radial section of redwood ×700. (b) Sections of natural fibres ×300. (c) Highly magnified grooves in a gramophone record. (d) X-ray photograph of a shell. (e) Electrical discharge. (f) *Biddulphia sinensis* ×100

11p

NATURAL GAS

O'Brien J. F. *Design by Accident* Dover, N.Y., 1968.

Rottger E. *Creative Paper Craft* Batsford, London, 1970.

Slides of many source materials are available from the following firms.

A. Clarkson, 338 High Holborn, London W.C.2.

Dr. Block Color Productions, 1309 North Genesee Avenue, Hollywood, California 46, U.S.A.

The Miniature Gallery, 60 Rushett Close, Long Ditton, Surrey.

Looking and Seeing Filmstrips, 81 Southway, London N. 20.

A good designer will always try to cultivate both an enquiring mind and an alert eye, able to see unusual combinations of ideas and sources.

In *Figure 13.5* will be seen simple design units based on some of the sources already illustrated. This type of unit can be arranged either as part of a regular repeat or all-over pattern, or each separate unit can be combined or enlarged to form the basis of a large printed or batik hanging.

Repeat patterns

Any shape or line, if repeated many times, will give some form of pattern. It is the manner of the repeat that varies the pattern and produces the complexity of the overall result, however simple the original unit. Often the shapes produced between the repeating units become more dominant than the units themselves.

There are two main ways of forming a repeat pattern: regular, rhythmic building up of balancing structures, repeating at measured and equal intervals; and irregular, or random, construction.

Figure 13.4. Other design sources. (a) An early 19th century railway engine. (b) Screen print on cotton by Linje Heming for Saini Salonen, Sweden, 1967. (c) Letraset borders. (d) A printed circuit. (e) Postage stamp. (f) Flyovers at Los Angeles. (g) Screen print on cotton satin for Bernard Wardle, 1968

The basic forms of regular patterning (which are shown in *Figure 13.6*) consist of the square, brick or half-shift, half-drop, diamond, triangle, ogee, hexagon, and scale. These may be used all-over, in stripes (horizontal, vertical, or diagonal), alternately inverted, and in a wide variety of quarter, third and other drops and shifts and combinations.

In order to save time when planning a repeat pattern, it is

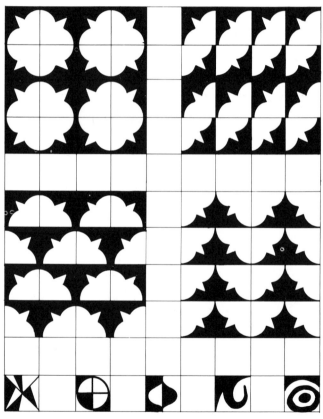

Figure 13.5. Design units based on some of the sources in *Figures 13.1* to *13.4*

sensible to prepare 16 identical units, cut out each, and experiment with different arrangements of shifts, drops and inverted stripes as suggested above or in the section on pad printing.

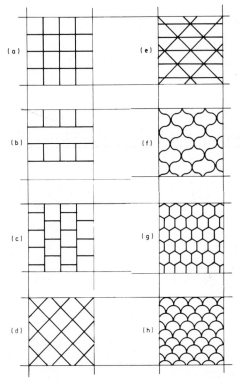

Figure 13.6. Basic forms of regular patterns. (a) Square. (b) Brick or half-shift. (c) Half-drop. (d) Diamond. (e) Triangle. (f) Ogee. (g) Hexagon. (h) Scale

If two mirrors are placed at right angles to each other as in *Figure 13.7* and the block of prints is placed in the angle, a much larger development of the overall linking possibilities of various arrangements will appear.

It is always useful to look at a design in a mirror; weaknesses or lack of balance in the basic design will show up in this unusual view.

Viewing the design through pieces of tinted cellophane or lighting gelatine will give some idea of the effect of the pattern on a coloured ground.

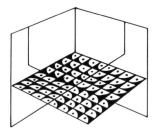

Figure 13.7. Using two mirrors to show one form of repeat

When printing all-over repeat patterns, it is best to make the unit fit into the fabric width, allowing 12 mm (½ in) selvedges (e.g., a 122 cm (48 in) wide fabric, after leaving selvedges, would permit unit sizes of 12 cm (4¾ in), 10 cm (4 in), 20 cm (8 in), 30 cm (12 in), and so on). Where this cannot be done, start from the centre of the fabric and work outwards to each selvedge. Lightly crease the centre line of the fabric rather than use a pencil mark, which may not wash out.

After the design is complete, it is still important not to look upon the chosen method of printing as a way of copying the design on to the fabric. The method should translate and alter the drawn or painted pattern according to the technique and type of fabric being used.

Hangings and decorative panels

It is essential for this form of decoration to be and to look a complete, independent design, satisfactory in its own right and not merely a piece cut off a repeat-patterned length. This criterion allows many possibilities. A few are shown in *Plate*

6, developing from basic units similar to those used in *Figure 13.5.*

Experiment with the shape or shapes as has been suggested for repeat patterning. Study rough drawings in the mirror. Use cut-out pieces of stiff card to see how the main areas will relate. Always hang up the design or look at it from above to see it as a whole.

A further unusual view is that shown by a distorting mirror. This can be of the circular, decorative type, or one made from mirror foil on a prepared backing, similar to the distorting mirrors used in fairs and amusement arcades.

The simplest and most adaptable method of making such a mirror is to glue or paste a piece of mirror foil on to a flexible piece of card. The card is pasted from the centre outwards and the foil applied, smoothing it from the centre outwards. Leave it flat to dry, making sure it is without bubbles or wrinkles, with a board placed on top to prevent warping. When it is dry, concave and convex shapes can be made by means of long veneer pins or nails set in a board to hold the card in various curvatures.

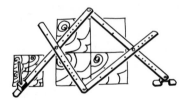

Figure 13.8. A pantograph

Such simple devices save a great deal of planning and tedious repetition. Another useful tool for copying, enlarging, or reducing a design when transferring it to fabric is a pantograph (*Figure 13.8*).

The finished print can be presented in a variety of ways. One of the simplest methods is as a banner, using either rods slipped through hems at top and bottom, or the slip-on hangers sold for posters.

Fabric can also be stretched over a simple wood frame, the corners of which are made with corner plates or corrugated metal joints and glued to give a flat, rectangular shape. Or it can be fixed on a stretcher such as is used for canvases for paintings. This gives a much lighter mounting than the more usual hardboard backing.

The mounted fabric can be placed on a larger, fabric-covered or painted backing board. However it is mounted, it can be framed with a simple box or other frame.

Colour

Of all the elements of design, colour is the most complex, individual, and personal. Many theories have been developed since renaissance man first looked objectively at the world and applied scientific thought to it. Leonardo da Vinci (1452–1519) already had a fairly accurate notion of opposing (contrasting) colours and colour gradation. He grouped polar colours into three entities: black/white, blue/yellow, and green/red. Sir Isaac Newton (1643–1727) and J. W. v. Goethe (1749–1832) propounded different theories, which were accepted by many scientists and artists until the present day. The chemist Wilhelm Ostwald (1853–1932) developed the ideas of Philipp Runge (1777–1810) into a comprehensive theory based on a double-ended cone with one tip white and the other black. Full colours occupied the middle 'equator' and all possible graduations and mixes were possible. This theory has been extensively used in art teaching. Among painters, the Impressionist Seurat attempted to break down light into separate dots of primary hues, and the Post-Impressionist Cézanne used pure colour. This was taken further by the De Stijl movement.

In more recent times, architects and designers have developed even more scientific theories, such as the German colour chart DIN6164 and the Ives, Munsell, and TGL systems.

It is often said that colour sense, like perfect pitch in music or the ability to draw with western pespective, is inborn and very difficult to acquire later in life. Too often, colour-schemes derived from Ostwald's or other theories are rather mechanical, 'pasty', or over-planned. This is similar to the mechanical, exaggerated effect given by mathematical perspective.

As in painting pictures, imitation may be flattering to the original artist, yet it rarely helps one to find one's own way of expression. Ideas employed by other designers are of use, but hard work, experiment, and a 'seeing eye' are necessary for self-expression. The beginner may find the following ideas of use when starting to develop a personal sense of colour.

Many designers use black and white and tones of grey for their preliminary roughs. Once the design is approved, it is translated into colours that reflect the original strengths and relationships of the black/grey/white design.

Others use tones or shades of one colour, such as blue. A lesson may be learned from a painter like Corot who, when using such a colour-scheme in a painting, would accentuate the richness of the blues with one tiny spot of bright red – e.g., a red cloak in a blue/green landscape.

Designing is often carried out in tissue paper or coloured cellophane, plastic, or scraps of old lighting gelatine. Over-laying different colours will give a good idea of the way in which prints superimposed upon each other give new mixes of colour. Felt markers can be used to give blacks and dark lines, dots, and shapes. Torn edges can be faithfully repro-duced in screen printing, particularly by the greaseproof-paper method of blocking out.

Just as a dye is often 'saddened' by the addition of a little of another dye, so colours are often improved with a drop of grey, white, black, or an opposite colour. In this manner, the colour becomes your own personal one instead of the manufacturer's standard hue. Do not overdo the addition but retain the strength of the original.

A number of terms are used to describe the characteristics of a colour. One is 'hue', which refers to the basic or pure colour. Of the various systems used, most include three primaries, (yellow, red, blue), three secondaries (orange, violet, green), and six intermediaries (yellow-orange, red-orange, red-violet, blue-violet, blue-green and yellow-green). These will give a standard colour wheel or circle of 12 basic hues.

Another term is 'value'. This refers to the lightness (added white) or darkness (added black) of a colour. Where white is added to a hue, the result is called a 'tint' and is higher in value than the original hue. If black is added to a hue, a 'shade' is produced, and this is lower in value than the original hue.

'Intensity' or 'chroma' describes the saturation of a hue in any colour.

With pigment colours, as in painting, white or an extender is added to give tints of higher values. With textile dyes, the same effect is obtained by adding water or a special extender supplied by the manufacturer. Most dyes or pigments tend to dry lighter and should be tried out before commencing a final piece of work.

Two other factors affect the final appearance of a colour: the texture of the fabric weave (ribbed, crash, fine, coarse, etc.) and that of the dye, if it is of the pigment type.

Sources of colour inspiration
The first and ever-present inspiration is that supplied by nature. Autumn and spring colours are obvious inspirations for design. It is often noticeable that good gardeners use grey foliage to set off brilliant hues, or plant related colours near to each other. Examine a plant, determine the proportion of the different shades, tones, and hues in that one plant, and prepare a colour sample with the colours in the same proportion as in nature. Then examine how a number of such plants growing together look in relation to the brilliant hues, the background shades, and the way in which they are related to each other. Use this balance of colour in your own design.

Similarly examine dried plants, seedheads, and pressed flowers for the subtle variations of neutral shades they show.

Use the sources listed earlier in this section but this time from the colour point of view.

Of particular interest are certain modern paintings, such as those of Mondrian, Ben Nicholson, Klee, Picasso, Braque, Kandinski, Chagall, and Rouault, as well as stained glass, either in its traditional form or in modern concrete and glass 'constructions'. Look at the proportion of colours in each composition. Look particularly at the way that the designer or artist has achieved the result, how he or she concentrated the colours, balanced a small brilliant hue with a large leaden mass, obtained recession, and so on.

Appendix 1

General suppliers

Fabrics

Emil Adler, 23 Hilfield Court, off Belsize Ave., London NW3
Cottons, cambrics, cheesecloth, silks, in 10 m (silks) or 20 m lengths or by the piece.

R. V. Bailey and Co. Ltd., 62 Mina Rd., Bristol, BS2 9XL
Cottons by the piece of about 50 m.

Hartley's Fabrics, Bankfield Mill, Greenfield Rd., Colne, Lancs
A wide variety of dress and household fabrics by the yard or metre.

Marsland Textiles, Jubilee Mount, West Lillands, Brighouse, West Yorks
A wide variety of dress and household fabrics by the yard.

Whaleys (Bradford) Ltd., Harris Court, Great Horton, Bradford, West Yorks, BD7 4EQ
An outstanding variety of cottons, linens, silks, etc., many ready prepared for dyeing or printing and supplied in lengths from 3 m upward.

Certain general suppliers, such as Dryad and Polyprint, supply short lengths of fabrics for dyeing and printing.

Equipment, dyes, etc.

Great Britain

E. J. Arnold, Butterley St., Leeds, LS10 1AX
Block and screen materials, fabrics, dye sticks, Fabraprint, screen printing ink.

Barlow Whitney Ltd., Coombe Rd., Neasden, London NW10
Electric wax kettles for batik.

Berol Ltd., Oldmeadow Rd., King's Lynn, Norfolk, PE30 4JR
Block printing materials, Fabricol, Fabritint colours.

Candlemakers Supplies, 28 Blythe Rd., London W14 0HA
Batik and tie-dye materials, Procion M dyes, direct, acid, and basic dyes.

Colour Craft (Elizabeth Lewis), 37 Woodlands Way, Tarporley, Cheshire
Dyes, chemicals and utensils.

Dryad, P.O. Box 38, Northgates, Leicester, LE1 9BU
Block and screen materials, Dylon dyes, Reeves Craft Dyes, Oil Fabric Inks, Manutex, fabrics.

Durham Chemical Distributors Ltd., 55/57 Glencall Rd., Peckham, London
Dyes of various types.

Dylon International Ltd., London SE26 5AD
Dylon Cold Water Dyes, Color-Fun All-Fabric Paint, Liquid and Multi-Purpose Fabric Dyes, Ultra-Batik Dyes, Dygon.

General Tape Ltd., 26 Orphanage Rd, Birmingham B24 9T
Waterproof self-adhesive cloth tape for masking screen edges.

George Hall (Sales) Ltd., Hardman St, Chestergate, Stockport SK3 0HA
Screen printing materials and pigment colours.

T. N. Lawrence & Son Ltd., 2–4 Bleeding Heart Yard, Greville St., Hatton Garden, London EC1N 8SL
Block printing materials and oil fabric inks, books.

London Textile Workshop, 65 Rosebery Rd., London N10
Natural, acid, direct and reactive dyes, synthetic indigo, Manutex.

Polyprint, 815 Lisburn Rd, Belfast, N. Ireland, BT9 7GX
Screen printing materials, Polyprint colours, fabrics.

Reeves, P.O. Box 91, Wealdstone, Harrow, HA3 5QN
Block printing materials, Oil Fabric Inks.

George Rowney & Co. Ltd., P.O.Box 10, Bracknell, Berkshire, RG12 4ST
Block printing materials, screen and fabric printing colours.

Royal Schoeten-Harig (Trading) Ltd. Moss Lane Trading Estate, Moss Lane, Whitefield, Manchester 25 6FH
Nafka gum.

Selectasine Serigraphics Ltd., 65 Chislehurst Rd., Chislehurst, Kent, BR7 5NP

Screen printing materials, fabrics, fabric inks, Helizarin pigment dye colours.

Sericol Group Ltd., 24 Parsons Green Lane, London SW6 4HS

Screen printing materials, e.g. Texiscreen and Texical.

Gordon Slater Ltd., Crown St., Chester Rd., Manchester 15

Nafka gum.

Textile Bookshop (Andrea Jeavons), Tynwald Mills, St. Johns, Isle of Man

Books and magazines on textiles.

Winsor & Newton, Wealdstone, Harrow, A3 5RH

Block and screen printing materials, Printex.

U.S.A.

Advance International, 402 N. Noble St., Chicago, ILL 60622

Aqua-Set Screen Fabric Inks, Pigment Colours, fabrics, etc.

Arts and Crafts Materials Corp., 321 Park Ave, Baltimore 1, MD.

Batik, block and screen materials, fabrics, dyes, etc.

Craft-Tool Co., 1 Industrial Road, Wood-Ridge, N.J. 07075

Batik, block and screen materials, fabrics, dyes, etc.

Dharma Trading Co., P.O. Box 1288, Berkeley, CA 94701

Batik and tie-dye materials, dyes, fabrics, etc.

Fibrec Inc., 2815 Eighteenth St., San Francisco, CA 94110

Batik materials, dyes, etc.

Geigy Chemical Co., P.O. Box 430, Yonkers, N.Y.

Tinolite pigment dyestuffs.

Hunt Manufacturing Co., 1405 Locust St., Philadelphia 19102

Screen fabric inks, etc.

Kelco Co., 75 Terminal Ave., Clark, N.J.

Keltex.

Siphon Art, 74D Hamilton Dr., Ignacio, CA 94947

Batik pigment colours, Dorlands Textile Wax Resist, Versatex textile paint, Versatex air brush ink.

Canada

Fibre Factory Ltd., 1745 Marine Drive, West Vancouver, B.C. V7V 1J5

Dyes.

Appendix 2

Selected bibliography

This list consists of practical books; those containing some historical information are marked with an asterisk.

Bolton, E. *Lichens for Vegetable Dyeing* Studio.

Clarke W. *An Introduction to Textile Printing* Newnes-Butterworth/I.C.I., London, latest edition.

Davenport E. *Yarn Dyeing* Sylvan Press, London.

Johnston M. P. and Kaufman G. *Design on Fabrics* Reinhold, N.Y., 1967.

Krevitsky N. *Batik Art and Craft* Reinhold, N.Y., 1964.

Maile A. *Tie-and-Dye as a Present-Day Craft* Mills & Boon, London/Taplinger, N.Y., 1963.

Palmer J. *Dyeing with Natural Dyes* Thorsons, 1980.

Ponting K. *A Dictionary of Dyes and Dyeing* Mills & Boon, London, 1980.

Robertson S. *Dyes from Plants* Van Nostrand–Reinhold, N.Y., 1973

Robinson S. *A History of Dyed and Printed Textiles* Visual Publications, London, rev. ed. 1977. (Sets of transparencies with detailed notes.)

Russ S. *Fabric Printing by Hand* Studio Vista, London, 1964.

Storey J. *Manual of Dyes and Fabrics* Thames & Hudson, London, 1978.

Storey J. *Manual of Textile Printing* Thames & Hudson, London, 1974.

Thurstan V. *The Use of Vegetable Dyes* Dryad Press, Leicester, latest edition.

Appendix 3

Organisations and courses

For a full descriptive and illustrated list of the textile collections in museums in Canada, France, Great Britain, Ireland, and the U.S.A., please consult the very comprehensive volumes by Cecil Lubell, Studio Vista, London; Cassell & Collier, Macmillan, London; Van Nostrand Reinhold N.Y. 1976–1978. They are also excellent source books for design.

For information on courses on aspects of practical work in textiles, application may be made in Great Britain to the following.

The Crafts Council, 8 Waterloo Place, London SW1Y 4AT, who publish *Crafts* magazine which, as well as informative articles on aspects of all crafts, also contains advertisements and notices of courses, exhibitions, and suppliers.

The Design Centre, 28 Haymarket, London SW1Y 4SY has frequent exhibitions of contemporary textiles and a consumer design index.

Devon Centre for Further Education, Dartington College of Arts, Totnes, Devon.

Eliza Leadbetter, Rookery College, Whitegate, Northwich, Cheshire.

London Textile Workshop, 65 Rosebery Rd, London N.10.

Styal Workshop, Quarry Bank Mill, Styal, Cheshire.

West Dean College of Craft Education, West Dean, Chichester, Sussex.

In the United States, information should be obtained from:

The American Craftsmen's Council, 16 East 52nd St., New York, N.Y., who publish *Craft Horizons*, which contains details of courses, exhibitions, and suppliers.

Davis Publications, Inc., Printers' Building, Worcester, Mass. publish the most useful magazine, *School Arts*.

Appendix 4

Screen-Master process

In this new process an original collage or design is used. It is essential that the collage or drawn design should be prepared with carbon-based materials such as soft pencils, Indian ink, special print pens, pieces cut from newspapers or magazines, instant lettering and designs etc. Designs may be made on soft overhead projector film.

The original design is placed face-up between the screen film and a backing sheet and this sandwich put in a special 'carrier sheet', which is then progressively fed through an Image Processor with flash exposures at each stage. This machine is operated by mains electricity and processes the stencils in a few seconds. As the material used is extremely sensitive it will reproduce anything from pen and ink to the half-tones of newspaper photographs.

After completion, the stencil material is ready for stretching on the screen printing frame. This can be done with double-sided adhesive tape, masking tape or staples. The stencil material should be attached with the mesh side uppermost so that it will be in contact with the fabric when printing. The stencil should be stretched as tightly as possible. The screen is then ready to print. After a few test prints inspect the screen for pinholes and touch out with a special blue correction fluid.

The recommended screen inks are specially formulated for use on natural and man-made fabrics. They are water-based, non-toxic and intermixable. When dry, after approximately 15 min, the fabric should be ironed through cotton or paper for one minute on both sides at about 135°C or as appropriate for the fabric used.

Gold, silver and clear powders are also available for sprinkling, before fixing, on wet prints. Inks etc. are washed up in clean, cold water. Free decorative treatment may be added by the use of fabric paints directly from small plastic bottles fitted with fine line adaptors.

All the necessary materials for this process are obtainable from Dryad of Leicester.

'Print Gocco' Instant Stencil Multicolour Printer

Although intended, in the main, for the production of low-cost, high-quality, multicolour prints on paper or card, this process can be used for single prints on fabric with are fixed, when dry, by ironing on both sides through cotton or paper.

The design is prepared and placed in the printer where it is 'engraved' on a stencil with a battery operated flash unit. Special coloured inks are then applied to the stencil which is inserted in the printer together with the fabric. By depressing the printer handle, the design is printed in the various colours used.

Two sizes of printer are available, as well as a variety of accessories, from Dryad of Leicester.

Index